# Growing Up Royal

## LIFE IN THE SHADOW OF THE BRITISH THRONE

BY JANE BILLINGHURST

ANNICK PRESS

TORONTO + NEW YORK + VANCOUVER

We acknowledge the support of the Canada Council for the Arts, the Ontario Arts Council, and the Government of Canada through the Book Publishing Industry Development Program (BPIDP) for our publishing activities.

Edited by Barbara Pulling
Copy-edited by Elaine Jones
Proofread by Elizabeth McLean
Cover and interior design by Irvin Cheung/iCheung Design
Cover photograph by Jayne Fincher/Photographers International
All interior photographs by Photographers International unless otherwise stated

**Cataloguing in Publication Data**

Billinghurst, Jane, 1958–
      Growing up royal : life in the shadow of the British throne

Includes index.
ISBN 1-55037-623-3 (bound)    ISBN 1-55037-622-5 (pbk.)

1. Kings and rulers — Children — Juvenile literature. I. Title.
HQ781.B54 2001    j305.23    C2001-930209-6

The text was typeset in Perpetua, Fontesque & Meta.

Printed and bound in Canada

| **Distributed in Canada by** | **Distributed in the U.S.A. by** | **Published in the U.S.A. by** |
| --- | --- | --- |
| Firefly Books Ltd. | Firefly Books (U.S.) Inc. | Annick Press (U.S.) Ltd. |
| 3680 Victoria Park Avenue | P.O. Box 1338 | |
| Willowdale, ON | Ellicott Station | |
| M2H 3K1 | Buffalo, NY 14205 | |

visit us at **www.annickpress.com**

To my parents, who did not bring me up royal
but did a good job anyway.

# Contents

# Introduction

HAVE YOU EVER WOKEN UP one morning hating your life and wishing you could be someone else? Perhaps you have imagined that who you are is all a big mistake, and you were really meant to be born into a family that was fabulously wealthy. Then you would have servants to do your every bidding. You would shop in the best stores. You would go to wonderful parties. You would spend your vacations at posh ski resorts or on sun-drenched beaches on secluded tropical islands. Heads would turn wherever you went.

Who lives that kind of life these days? You could be a movie star, of course, but then you're only as good as your latest movie. What if you end up being cast in a real bomb? You could be a member of a rich family. That's better. Still, there's no guarantee family squabbles won't fritter away the fortune, and money does not always bring social standing. No, if you want it all — wealth, power, and image — nothing beats being born royal.

Imagine you are a prince or a princess. Your home is an enormous stone castle with turrets and steep winding staircases. Each morning when you are woken up, you throw open a wardrobe full of designer outfits. There are soft woolens and crisp cottons, all in your favorite styles and colors. Servants pad quietly into your room to ask what you would like to do today. Over a leisurely breakfast, you decide whether to take the dogs for a brisk walk through your private woodlands or to call for your fishing rod and a picnic lunch so you can try your luck in the river that flows through the royal estate. If you have time, you could check out the royal farm to see how the pigs are fattening up, summon the royal Rolls Royce for a drive into town, or invite someone famous to tea. In the evenings there are dignitaries to meet, movie premieres to attend, and ribbons to cut. For special occasions you wear glittering jewels or medals and fur-trimmed velvet robes. Everywhere you go, people line up to meet you. Newspapers write about you. People admire you. You are born royal.

There are no auditions to be born royal, no interviews, and no elections. You don't have to take any tests or possess any particular talents. All you have to do is show up in the right family at the right time. No doubt you're thinking that with castles to live in, closets full of clothes to choose from, and carriages to ride in for those extra-special occasions, royal life has got to be the most wonderful life in the world. But are you right? What is it really like to be born a prince or a princess these days? Let's take a closer look and see.

# ONE

# What Does It Mean to Be Royal?

THE ONLY WAY TO BECOME ROYAL is either to be born into a royal family or to marry into one. We'll take it as a given that you're too young to marry, so being born into a royal family would definitely be the way to go. There are ten royal families left in Europe and twenty or so scattered in other countries of the world, including Bahrain, Bhutan, Brunei, Japan, Jordan, Kuwait, Lesotho, Malaysia, Morocco, Nepal, Oman, Qatar, Saudi Arabia, Swaziland, Thailand, Tonga, the United Arab Emirates, Wallis and Futuna, and Western Samoa. (Wow, that was quite a list!)

To make your choice more manageable, you could start by concentrating on European royals. There's an overview of your options in the section entitled "The Royal Families of Europe" at the back of this book. The number of families to choose from is not what it used to be, but European royal families had a hard time of it in the twentieth century. World wars, revolutions, and changes in political philosophy all took their toll. Empires crumbled, republics were born, and many royals were forced into exile. (Actually, those who made it into exile were the lucky ones. The Russian tsar and his family did not make it out of their country alive: they were shot by revolutionaries in 1918.) As a result of all this upheaval, there are a number of princes and princesses in Europe today who have inherited titles but have no thrones to go with them.

Feel free to browse through the European families listed, but if you're seriously considering this royal business, you might as well aim for the big time. The grandest royal family in Europe today, and the one

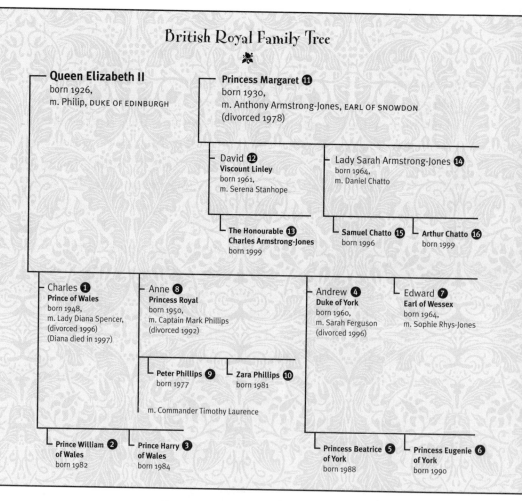

# British Royal Family Tree

**Queen Elizabeth II**
born 1926,
m. Philip, DUKE OF EDINBURGH

**Princess Margaret** ⓫
born 1930,
m. Anthony Armstrong-Jones, EARL OF SNOWDON
(divorced 1978)

**David** ⓬
**Viscount Linley**
born 1961,
m. Serena Stanhope

**Lady Sarah Armstrong-Jones** ⓮
born 1964,
m. Daniel Chatto

**The Honourable** ⓭
**Charles Armstrong-Jones**
born 1999

**Samuel Chatto** ⓯
born 1996

**Arthur Chatto** ⓰
born 1999

**Charles** ❶
**Prince of Wales**
born 1948,
m. Lady Diana Spencer,
(divorced 1996)
(Diana died in 1997)

**Anne** ❽
**Princess Royal**
born 1950,
m. Captain Mark Phillips
(divorced 1992)

**Andrew** ❹
**Duke of York**
born 1960,
m. Sarah Ferguson
(divorced 1996)

**Edward** ❼
**Earl of Wessex**
born 1964,
m. Sophie Rhys-Jones

**Peter Phillips** ❾
born 1977

**Zara Phillips** ❿
born 1981

m. Commander Timothy Laurence

**Prince William** ❷
**of Wales**
born 1982

**Prince Harry** ❸
**of Wales**
born 1984

**Princess Beatrice** ❺
**of York**
born 1988

**Princess Eugenie** ❻
**of York**
born 1990

The numbers beside the names indicate who is next in line for the throne.
For instance, Prince William is second in line behind his father, Prince Charles.

that attracts most attention, is the British royal family. Queen Elizabeth II has been the sovereign of the United Kingdom of Great Britain and Ireland since 1952, and she doesn't show signs of giving up any time soon. The heir to the British throne is Charles, Prince of Wales, who is now well into middle age. The heir to the heir is his oldest son, Prince William, who turned eighteen in the year 2000. Prince William has one brother, Prince Henry, who is two years younger.

At left is the family tree for Queen Elizabeth II and her family. All the Queen's children are princes and princesses, and so are her grandchildren William, Henry (called Harry), Beatrice, and Eugenie. The children of Princess Margaret, the Queen's sister, and those of the Queen's daughter, Princess Anne, are *not* princes and princesses, though. The reason for this is that titles are passed down the male line, so unless princesses marry princes, they do not pass their titles on to their children. Princess Margaret's former husband, Anthony Armstrong-Jones, accepted the title Earl of Snowdon when he married into the royal family, ensuring that his son is a viscount and his daughter a lady. Princess Anne's first husband, Captain Mark Phillips, did not want a title, so her children are just plain Peter and Zara.

When Prince Charles becomes king, he will likely be King Charles III, and when Prince William succeeds his father, he will be King William V. (New kings and queens get to choose which of their names they want to use, so these are only guesses.) Both Edward VIII and his younger brother George VI are examples of British kings who chose formal names different from the names they used at home. Edward VIII, whose full name was Edward Albert Christian George Andrew Patrick David — which is quite a mouthful — was always called by his last name, David. George VI, who was Albert Fredrick Arthur George, was always known

# The Powers of King William V

As of the year 2001, if Prince William were to ascend the throne of Britain, he would be king of the United Kingdom of Great Britain and Northern Ireland and all the countries in the Commonwealth that recognize the British king or queen as their sovereign: Antigua and Barbuda, Australia, The Bahamas, Barbados, Belize, Canada, Grenada, Jamaica, New Zealand, Papua New Guinea, St. Christopher and Nevis, St. Lucia, St. Vincent and the Grenadines, the Solomon Islands, and Tuvalu. He would also be head of Britain's armed forces, head of the Church of England, and head of the Commonwealth. As sovereign he would preside at ceremonial occasions, visit local communities, and represent Britain around the world. He would also have powers that he would exercise on the advice of his government. These include the power to open Parliament and give royal assent to Parliamentary bills, proclamations, and orders-in-council; appoint and consult with prime ministers; dissolve Parliament and call for new elections; appoint and dismiss judges; pardon criminals; declare war or peace; confer peerages and knighthoods; grant awards for gallantry or distinguished service; and tell members of the royal family under the age of twenty-five whom they may or may not marry. This sounds impressive, but as a constitutional monarch, he'll do most of these things only if the government of the day wants him to.

as Bertie. Queen Elizabeth II — who grew up as Princess Elizabeth — didn't hold with confusing people. When she was asked what name she would be taking as queen, she said, "My own name, of course — what else?"

The British royal family, like all the European royal families that have survived into the twenty-first century, is a constitutional, rather than an absolute, monarchy. So if you thought being born royal would mean you could summon your guards with a snap of your fingers and have them chop off the heads of people who annoy you, forget it. Gone are the days when European kings and queens could impose laws, dismiss politicians they didn't like, and raise armies to impose their will upon the land. European royals today exercise only as much power as their people are prepared to give them. Nowadays it is the politicians — the elected representatives of the people — who get to make all the big decisions. European royals cannot openly support one political party over another or even make remarks that seem to do so, nor can they hold elected office. If you think about it, it makes sense for royals to stay out of political debates. Politicians are voted in and out of office as people change their minds. In giving up their rights to meddle in politics, royal families have ensured that no matter who is in government, the royal family will retain its position at the top of the social heap. This means that although people will be impressed by your social position, they don't have to do everything you say just because you are a king or a queen (or a prince or a princess).

Even if European royal families can no longer throw their weight around the way they used to, there are still lots of things they can do. As a member of a royal family, you can keep up to date on current events and get important people together in one place to discuss them. You may not be able to command anyone's presence, but people certainly think long and hard before turning down an invitation to a royal tea. All you have to do is sit down and write a bunch of impressive-looking invitations.

In 1984, Britain's Prince Charles brought together wealthy business people and young black leaders from deprived inner-city areas. The prince made a keynote speech and then his guests talked — for two days. At the end of the conference, the leaders of industry said they had

had no idea there was so much talent among the black leadership, and the inner-city leaders said they had not expected such understanding of their problems from big business. The result was a major step forward in the country's race relations.

A royal family can also make an enormous difference in how people treat one another. If you are wise, you can use your royal influence to do a lot of good. Take diseases, for instance. When Queen Elizabeth II and Prince Philip of Britain visited a leper colony in Nigeria on a royal tour in 1956 and shook the hand of a young leper, the supervisor of the settlement was thrilled. He knew that news of the visit would be broadcast around the world, so this simple handshake would go a long way toward convincing people that most of their fears of the disease were groundless.

As a royal, you can also lend your support to any number of charities. Your name on an organization's letterhead will help with fundraising appeals, and the promise of your presence at gala events will ensure brisk ticket sales. There's nothing like a tiara or two to brighten up a social event. Charles's sister, Princess Anne, campaigns tirelessly and travels widely to promote such charities as Save the Children and Riding for the Disabled.

If you have a palace at your disposal, you can raise even more money. In 2000, Wimbledon heroes Bjorn Borg and John McEnroe were invited to recreate their classic championship finals of 1980 and 1981 on the tennis court at Buckingham Palace, Queen Elizabeth II's London home. The money raised went to Full Stop, a campaign to put an end to cruelty to children.

All of us, at times, need people to look up to, and royals — when they are behaving well — can give their subjects role models to admire.

Queen Elizabeth the Queen Mother (Prince William's great grand-mother) is a testament to the uplifting effect royalty can have. During the Second World War, she refused to leave Buckingham Palace even though the Germans were dropping bombs on London. When the palace was hit, she said she was glad, because it meant she now had something in common with other Londoners whose homes had been bombed. Her courage inspired the British people and may well have hastened the end of the war.

As a royal, you also perform duties on behalf of the country you represent. The awards and recognition given by a royal family — knighthoods, for instance — honor people who have served their country well. A certificate or plaque is always nice, but a ceremony with the queen produces a special thrill. (When Prince Charles was lit-tle he once practiced this skill at tea time by knighting his footman, Richard, with a butter knife when Richard stooped down to pick up something Charles had dropped.)

Royals also work hard at making people feel better. When Prince Charles's wife, Princess Diana, comforted a patient in hospital or knelt down to shake a child's hand in a crowd, she gave these people a moment they would remember for the rest of their lives.

Finally, just going about your traditional royal business with birthdays, coronations, weddings, and the occasional Silver Jubilee will pull in the tourists and give everyone an excuse to party. When Charles and Diana got married in 1981, people the world over stopped what they were doing and tuned in to watch the fairy-tale princess marry her prince.

King George III of Britain once said that royals should "be seen, be splendid." His ancestors, including the current British queen,

Queen Elizabeth II, have clearly agreed with him. Of all the royal families in Europe, the British royal family is the one that has retained most of the trappings we associate with royalty — colorful parades with horses and carriages, lots of servants in fancy clothes, and strict rules of royal etiquette. To help you decide if being royal is really all that it's cracked up to be, let's take a behind-the-scenes look at what their life of splendor is really like.

# TWO

# In the
# Palace Nursery

WHEN YOU ARE BORN into a royal family, you can expect an enthusiastic reception. The birth of a new child is a time for rejoicing in any family; children are especially important in royal families because they are the only way to continue the family tradition of ruling the country. Even if your parents don't go quite as far as the grandfather of the current king of Spain, who presented his newborn daughter to then-king Alfonso XIII on a silver platter, they will be very happy that you have arrived.

Be aware that whether you are born a boy or a girl can make a big difference to your chances of inheriting your country's throne. Belgium, the Netherlands, and Sweden are the most progressive European countries in this regard. In each of these countries, the oldest child inherits the throne, regardless of sex. After the next generation, this will also be the case in Norway. Next on the list are Britain, Denmark, Monaco, and Spain, where girls inherit the throne only if they have no brothers. (Queen Elizabeth has allowed that there might be room for discussion of the rules in Britain, but the issue has not been considered pressing, because the next four individuals in line for the throne — Prince Charles, Prince William, Prince Harry, and

Charles's brother Andrew — are all male.) In two European states — Liechtenstein and Luxembourg — the situation is even more dire. Girls inherit only if there are no eligible males in *any* branch of the family. You may want to keep these rules in mind when you are considering which royal family you'd like to be born into.

No matter what your sex, your subjects will certainly be anxious to hear all about you. A crowd of thousands was waiting outside Buckingham Palace when Britain's Prince Charles was born. When a policeman rushed across the courtyard with the news that the baby was a boy, the people outside the palace gates erupted into noisy cheers. Later that day a royal salute of forty-one guns was fired. Bonfires burned around the country and more gun salutes were fired around the world. The bells of Westminster Abbey in London rang for six hours straight, and flags were flown from public buildings. For a week, the water in the fountains in London's Trafalgar Square was illuminated by blue floodlights.

(Don't be disappointed if your royal parents, ecstatic though they may be, are less in awe of you than your loyal subjects are. Prince Philip thought Prince Charles looked rather like a plum pudding when he was born. Prince Charles said of his firstborn, Prince William, "He really does look surprisingly appetizing and has sausage fingers just like mine.")

After your first few weeks as a brand-new royal, it will be time for you to be christened. This is an important event in Britain, since whoever rules the country is also the head of the Church of England. (Ever since the Roman Catholic king James II was run out of the country in 1688, the kings and queens of Britain have been firmly Protestant. The Queen's cousin Prince Michael of Kent gave up any chance of ever

# Royal Birth Watch

British queens used to give birth to their children with members of the British government looking on. This strange arrangement began because of the uneasy relationship between Protestants and Roman Catholics, which had been going on ever since the pope refused to grant King Henry VIII a divorce in 1533. In 1688, Mary Modena, the Roman Catholic wife of King James II, became pregnant. James had two Protestant daughters by his first wife, Anne. According to the rules of succession, if Mary gave birth to a son, the boy — who would be Catholic — would automatically be first in line for the throne.

When Mary did indeed give birth to a boy, powerful Protestants started a rumor that the baby had been smuggled into her bedroom in a warming pan. The British were not very keen on King James anyway, and within seven months of the boy's birth, the king and his family were forced to flee the country. (A warming pan, by the way, is a flattish round pan with a lid and a long wooden handle. British houses are notoriously damp and drafty. In the days before hot water bottles, a warming pan filled with hot water or hot coals would be slipped between the sheets to warm up the bed.)

Neither the next queen, Mary, nor her sister, Anne, who succeeded her, had any children who survived infancy. After Anne, Britain had five kings in succession, whose wives meekly accepted the government observers. When it was Queen Victoria's turn, she banished the government watchdogs to an adjoining room and reduced the party to one — the Home Secretary. Victoria was followed by four more kings, the last of whom, George VI, took pity on his daughter Princess Elizabeth (now Queen Elizabeth II) and changed the rules for royal births once again. Prince Charles became the first royal baby in over 250 years whose birth was not witnessed by a representative of the state. The Home Secretary was informed by telephone instead.

sitting on the British throne when he married a divorced Roman Catholic, Baroness Marie-Christine von Reibnitz, in 1978. He was sixteenth in line for the throne.)

British royal christenings are usually held in the music room overlooking the garden at Buckingham Palace. If the British royal family is your royal family of choice, there you'll be with your parents and your godparents. As in other families, your parents will choose your godparents for you, and there will likely be quite a lot of them. William and Harry each have six. William's include one princess (Princess Alexandra, the daughter of the Queen's cousin the Duke of Kent); one ex-king (King Constantine of Greece); and one famous philosopher and storyteller, the late Sir Laurens van der Post. Harry's six godparents include Princess Margaret's daughter, the former Lady Sarah Armstrong-Jones, now Lady Sarah Chatto; his uncle Prince Andrew; and Bryan Organ, an artist who has painted a number of royal portraits.

For the ceremony, each new baby in the British royal family is dressed in a cream-colored christening gown of satin and lace that was first worn by Queen Victoria's eldest son, Edward, in 1841. (The shoes are new each time, though, as every baby has different-sized feet.) The baptism takes place over a silver-gilt font shaped like a lily with open petals. It was designed by Queen Victoria's husband, Prince Albert, for the christening of their oldest daughter, Princess Vicky, in 1840. The water in the font is from the River Jordan. It's the same water John the Baptist used to baptize Christ. (Well, it's from the same river, anyway.) In 1981, when water supplies were running low, the Jordanian Embassy in London was thoughtful enough to send over a top-up for the christening of Princess Anne's daughter, Zara.

As a royal baby, the decision whether to cry or not will be up to you. Prince Charles was reported to have been "as quiet as a mouse," but in 1982 Prince William got hungry before the post-christening photo session and started to fuss. The only way his mother, Princess Diana, could keep him quiet was by giving him the end of her little finger to suck on. After his outburst, the press dubbed him "William, the Prince of Wails."

After the christening ceremony, a light lunch is served to the guests. In Queen Victoria's time, christenings were very lavish affairs. For her oldest son, Edward, the queen ordered a banquet with a cake that was nearly three meters (over eight feet) wide. To top it all off, there was a spectacular fireworks display. These days, though, the royal family has to be seen spending their money wisely, and royal christenings are elegant but relatively low key.

Your first official royal event successfully completed, it's time to start your royal life in earnest. The place where you'll spend most of your time for the next three years or so is the palace nursery.

When Prince William and Prince Harry were little, they lived in an apartment in Kensington Palace, which is close to Buckingham Palace in London. The boys had a nursery on the top floor above their parents' bedroom. They had one room to sleep in and another to play in. They also had a bathroom with a child-sized toilet and basin. Their nannies (they had two of them, a main nanny and an assistant), shared a bedroom-cum-living room on the same floor. William and Harry could see the royal helicopter pad from their nursery window, and one of William's first words was not "Mama" or "Dada" but "plane."

The boys were taken for walks around the palace's walled garden in a pram that once belonged to their father. When they were old enough to crawl, they had a sandbox and a swing behind the palace.

## William and Harry's Nannies

Old-fashioned royal nannies always wore starched nanny uniforms when they were on duty, but William and Harry's nanny Barbara Barnes wore her own clothes when she looked after the young princes. She was helped by an under-nanny, Olga Powell. When William traveled to Australia with his parents when he was just nine months old, Nanny Barnes came along, too. William and Harry's nannies got them up and dressed every morning, took them on outings, and had their meals with them in the nursery at Kensington Palace. With all the attention being heaped on William whenever he was out in public, he needed strict boundaries at home. Nanny Barnes, it seems, found it difficult to control her young charge, and when William was four, she left. Nanny Barnes was replaced by Ruth Wallace, known to the boys as "Nanny Roof." (She got her name because Harry was too young to be able to say "Ruth" properly.) It was hoped that Nanny Roof would instill some discipline into William, who had been embarrassing his parents with some of his behavior at public events. The change in nannies seemed to help and by the time he was five, William was well on his way to becoming the perfect little gentleman.

When they ventured outside the palace walls, they and their two nannies were accompanied by private detectives. Outings were encouraged, and William and Harry could enjoy ice-cream cones at the zoo just like other children. (Except, of course, most children don't have a bunch of grown-ups trailing them wherever they go.)

Because you are a royal child, your parents will likely not be able to spend much time with you. Their schedules will have been booked up to a year in advance, and they could have as many as 400 official engagements a year. When you think that there are only 365 days in a year, you can understand why it is they always seem so busy.

In your parents' absence, you will get to know your royal nannies very well. This could be a good thing or a bad thing, depending on the nanny. Don't think that just because you are royal you will necessarily be spared nasty nannies. Mrs. Green, who was hired by the future George V to care for his sons David (later Edward VIII) and Bertie (later George VI), was one of the nastiest ever.

Mrs. Green used to pinch little David before presenting him to his parents in the evenings. David, quite understandably, would cry, and his parents would wonder what they had done wrong. The nasty nanny would then whisk the little boy back to the nursery, where she would comfort him. Eventually she was found out and fired, but not before she had nearly starved David's younger brother Bertie. She would give Bertie his bottle and then take him for a vigorous walk in a bumpy pram so that very little of the milk was drunk. When Bertie was older, she would snatch away his food before he had a chance to touch it. The unfortunate boy was not very strong to begin with and suffered from digestive problems for the rest of his life.

In recent generations of British royals, parents have become more closely involved with their children's upbringing. Although she has been criticized for being a distant mother, Queen Elizabeth II did try to make room in her busy schedule for her children, Charles, Anne, Andrew, and Edward. When Prince Charles was young she reorganized her meetings with British prime minister Winston Churchill so that she could supervise her son's evening bath times. (She was careful to supervise from well out of splashing range, though.) Other than that, Charles saw very little of his parents. He would be presented to his mother for a brief half hour in the morning and then she'd try to spend an hour or two with him in the evening before he was put to bed.

(Not seeing much of your parents can make it difficult to keep on top of what is going on in the family. Charles was three when his mother, who up until then had been Princess Elizabeth, ascended the throne. He did not immediately realize what had happened. One day soon after moving into Buckingham Palace, he met one of the Queen's private secretaries in the corridor. Charles asked the man where he was going. "I'm going to see the Queen," the secretary replied. "Oh yes," said Charles. "Who's she?")

Not only did Queen Elizabeth not have much time for her children during the day, she also had to travel on business, sometimes taking very long trips. In 1953, she and Prince Philip left for a six-month tour of the Commonwealth, a loose association of former British colonies. Although the countries were now independent from Britain, they recognized the Queen as head of their association. At the end of the royal tour, five-year-old Charles and three-year-old Anne sailed out to Tobruk in North Africa on the royal yacht, *Britannia,* to meet their parents for the journey home. Charles could hardly contain his excitement at seeing his mother after such a long absence. But when he tried to push his way forward through the dignitaries to greet her, she said to him dismissively, "No, not you, dear," and started to work her way down the receiving line instead. Only when she had dispatched her royal obligations did she turn to greet her son.

Queen Elizabeth was a more experienced monarch and a slightly more hands-on mother by the time Andrew and Edward were born a decade later. When the nannies were having their night off, the Queen would occasionally babysit her sons. She would come with a page and a footman and have her supper on a tray with her feet up in front of the television.

One generation further on, Princess Diana was an even more involved mother, sometimes distressing the royal nannies because she took so much of the child-minding upon herself. She would rush to the children at night if they cried, which was considered "not done" for a member of the royal family. Charles, too, seemed delighted to be a father — at least in the early days. Once when the Prince and Princess of Wales were due to leave for an official engagement, Diana could not find Charles anywhere. She eventually tracked him down in the bath with William. The two princes were having a wonderful time and there was bath water all over the floor.

At this tender age as a royal you are too young to have any idea of what life holds in store, so no special behavior is called for. You can pretty much act like any active toddler, and no one will be too surprised.

When he traveled to Australia with his parents at the age of nine months, Prince William dumped the entire contents of a table set for tea onto the floor when he gave an experimental yank to the lace tablecloth. At the age of twelve months, he elicited an even more satisfying response when he pushed a bell in the nursery at Balmoral, the British royal retreat in Scotland. The bell summoned a large number of police and fire engines. (When he got a little older, William ran off with a fireman's helmet after a fire drill at Balmoral and refused to give it back.) Another of William's specialties as a toddler was breaking things. Whenever he got a new toy, his father would sigh: "Something else for him to smash." His most spectacular smash was of a scaled-down version of the car his parents were driving at the time. William drove his toy electric Jaguar XJ-S Cabriolet into the garage wall.

When William was not being destructive, he was much like any young boy. Although his mother did not allow him to watch violent shows on television, his toy collection included a huge arsenal of plastic guns. He climbed on the climbing frame in his backyard and ran around wearing his Spiderman outfit. At night, his parents would read to him in bed. Favorite books included Rudyard Kipling's *Just So Stories*.

Prince Charles had also caused trouble when he was young, although his misdeeds tended to be of a gentler nature than William's. In Buckingham Palace, there was a bell Queen Elizabeth could push if she wanted to see Charles's nanny. One day the bell rang and the nanny presented herself to the Queen, who said that she had not summoned her. The nanny went back to the nursery. The bell rang again. For a second time, the nanny came down to see the Queen, only to be told that she hadn't been called for. Nanny and the Queen then spied the young prince riding his pedal car down the corridor. Not only was he suspiciously close to the bell in question, they discovered he had just had an earnest conversation with the palace electrician about what each of the bells was for.

Don't expect that because you are royal you will be exempt from punishment if you misbehave. Even young royals soon learn that their actions have consequences. Queen Victoria's oldest daughter, Vicky, was reportedly quite a handful. When Princess Vicky insisted on calling the doctor "Brown" rather than "Dr. Brown," her mother told her that if she did it again, she would be sent to bed. When the doctor arrived the next morning, Vicky said, "Good morning, Brown." When her mother caught her eye, the little princess added, "And good night, Brown, for I am going to bed."

William and Harry's cousin Princess Beatrice was told off by her mother, Sarah, Duchess of York, when she stuck her tongue out and made a rude noise at a chipmunk cartoon character at Disneyland in

California. The next day at Sea World in San Diego, one of the aquarium's star attractions, a 225-kilogram (500-pound) sea lion called Clyde, stuck his tongue out at Princess Beatrice. She turned to her mother and said: "He's stuck his tongue out. He's naughty, isn't he?"

Whether there are consequences or not, some children just cannot resist temptation. William's uncle Prince Andrew had a reputation for misbehaving, and his parents were not averse to others taking him in hand when necessary. Once Andrew annoyed the grooms at the Royal Mews (the place where the royal horses and carriages are kept) so much that they threw him into a pile of manure. Although Andrew was seen running off to tell his mummy, none of the grooms got into trouble.

And, finally, remember that royal misbehavior can drive royal parents, like any parents, to distraction. When William was on an outing at Highgrove — his father's country estate — he started complaining that his hands were cold. His father responded tersely, "I told you to bring gloves when we left the house, and you didn't, so shut up."

THREE

# Realizing
# You're Different

IT'S A GRADUAL PROCESS, but some day soon after your
royal toddlerhood ends, you will begin to realize that you are in some
way different from other children. Prince Charles said: "I didn't wake up
in my pram one day and say, 'Yippee!' I think it's something that dawns
on you with the most ghastly, inexorable sense."

One of the tip-offs might be the gifts people give you. Sometimes
it is the sheer volume of them that is remarkable. When Prince Charles
was born, he received nearly one and a half tonnes (tons) of diapers
from the United States. When his parents returned from their six-
month tour of the Commonwealth, they came home laden with nearly
three tonnes of presents they had accumulated from well-wishers along
the way.

Other times it's the gifts themselves that provide the clue you
don't come from an ordinary family. Prince Charles said the best gift he
ever received was a working model of the Rock of Gibraltar, accurate
down to the last house. Clockwork trains ran through a tunnel, the
dockyards were equipped with electrically operated cranes, there were
model aircraft on the airfield, and the tiny model houses could be lit up
at night. Also from Gibraltar, Princess Anne was given a doll's bungalow

equipped with electricity. It was 2 meters long, 1.2 meters high, and 0.6 meters wide (7 feet by 4 feet by 2 feet), and the princess could crawl right inside it. Charles also had a three-masted schooner, big enough that he could get aboard.

A favorite with sisters Princess Elizabeth and Princess Margaret was *Y Bwthyn Bach* or The Little House, a gift to Princess Elizabeth on her sixth birthday from the people of Wales. This little thatched cottage, just the right size for a six-year-old, was constructed close by Royal Lodge in Windsor Park. The windows opened, and the cottage had plumbing, a radio that worked, and electric lights you could turn on and off. When she was little, Queen Elizabeth's daughter, Anne, used to lock herself in it when she and Charles quarreled. Charles would be left outside, kicking at the front door.

Prince William and Prince Harry also often received scaled-down versions of adult possessions as gifts. One day, after a trip to the Metropolitan Police's Special Escort Group headquarters in Barnes, southwest London, they both came back with mini–police uniforms complete with helmets and gloves. Sometimes the miniature gifts are much more expensive than this. Prince William received a scaled-down replica of his father's green Aston Martin V8 Volante. William's car wasn't as fast as his father's, but it could reach the impressive speed of sixty-five kilometers (forty miles) per hour. Barry Manilow, the singer, gave William's little brother Harry a twelve-centimeter (five-inch) antique baby piano as a christening gift. Neither of these gifts came close, however, to the present Princess Caroline's daughter, Charlotte of Monaco, got for her fifth birthday from her grandparents — an island off the coast of Italy valued at $7 million. (It would be like getting a mini-country all your own, I guess.)

But if you're imagining yourself in the British royal family, don't be surprised if, amid all these dazzling gifts, many of the toys in your royal nursery are hand-me-downs. Despite the family's immense wealth, the British royals can be amazingly frugal in their private lives. The Queen is said to walk the corridors of Buckingham Palace at night switching off unnecessary lights, and lost items are searched for rather than automatically replaced. One day young Charles was walking his dog on the royal estate of Sandringham in Norfolk. When he returned to the house, he had the dog but not the leash. He was told that leashes cost money and was sent right back out to find it.

The tradition of frugality has been passed on to the latest generation of British royals. When the boys were young, Prince Harry often wore Prince William's outgrown clothes, and William and Harry used to play with a set of wooden soldiers that once belonged to Prince Charles. Hand-me-down elephants were also popular items. William got to play with the same blue elephant that his father, Charles, had used when he was learning to walk, and Princess Beatrice inherited a huge pink rocking elephant that once belonged to her father, Prince Andrew. (Obviously the family is not big on garage sales. Imagine what they could get if they set up tables on their driveway to sell off their old household items.)

Another thing that might tip you off to your privileged position is all those servants who keep following you around. When Prince Charles was three, he was assigned his own personal footman, a man called Richard. When Charles went to tea with another little boy, he was puzzled. "Why haven't you got a Richard?" he asked his friend.

(If you were ever to become the king or queen of England, one of the servants you could employ would be a Royal Herb Strewer. In

1660, a woman called Bridget Rumny was paid $53 a year to accompany Charles II on his travels around the country. In those days there were open sewers in the streets, and people threw their slops out of windows. Needless to say, towns were incredibly smelly. The herb strewer's job was to throw about fragrant herbs, such as mint and lavender, to hide the stench. No herb strewers have been employed since 1821, but if you got as far as the throne and liked the idea of being accompanied by beautiful smells, you could always call on the senior unmarried daughter of the Fellowes family, who holds the rights to this position.)

When William and Harry were old enough not to need nannies any more, their father hired Tiggy Legge-Bourke to be their companion. Ms. Legge-Bourke (now Mrs. Pettifer) was not your typical child-minder. The boys spent a lot of their time on royal estates in the country, enjoying the traditional hunting, shooting, and fishing life of the British aristocracy, so it was useful to have someone around who knew how to skin a rabbit and gut a stag. "I give the princes what they need," Ms. Legge-Bourke said, "fresh air, a rifle, and a horse."

Being a royal can be lonely at times, and often it is your personal servants who know you best. When Queen Elizabeth was only nine months old and still a princess, a woman named Margaret Macdonald was hired as a nursery maid. The two became very close — even sharing a bedroom. "Bobo" Macdonald stayed in the royal employ, working as the Queen's dresser until she retired shortly before her death in 1993.

Nannies continue to exert an influence later in life. Even today, when something goes wrong, Queen Elizabeth has been heard to mutter, "Oh, nanny will be cross." Prince Charles grew very close to the family nanny, Mabel Anderson, sending her an invitation to his twenty-first birthday party and inviting her back to look after his own

# Royal Servants

Once Prince William becomes king, he will have a number of servants to attend to him. Here are some of the people who look after the royal family today.

**Crown Equerry:** The Crown Equerry looks after all the royal cars and carriages, and trains royal horses for ceremonial parades.

**Dressers:** Dressers look after the royal wardrobes.

**Equerries:** Equerries are personal assistants and companions to members of the royal family. Equerries are always men, and they always come from the armed forces. Their female counterparts are called ladies-in-waiting.

**Footmen:** Footmen are messengers, meeters and greeters of guests, servers of royal meals, and walkers of royal dogs. They also ride on royal carriages in royal parades and wait on senior members of the royal household. For everyday, they wear black tail coats and pants, with scarlet waistcoats trimmed with gold braid. For special occasions, they wear scarlet coats and waistcoats decorated with gold braid, pink stockings, and black buckle shoes.

**Gentleman Ushers:** Originally ushers ushered visitors into the sovereign's presence. Now they make visitors feel special at royal parties and help with crowd control at the palace on state occasions.

**Keeper of the Privy Purse:** The Keeper of the Privy Purse looks after the royal money (which is important since royals don't usually carry money about with them and are often a bit vague about what it is worth).

**Ladies-in-Waiting:** Ladies-in-waiting are assistants and companions to female members of the royal family. They are personally appointed by the Queen and work on a voluntary basis.

**Ladies of the Bedchamber:** Ladies of the Bedchamber are ladies-in-waiting who wait on the Queen at public engagements and state visits abroad. They supply hankies, collect bouquets of flowers, and make pleasant conversation with guests. They wear their own clothes to royal occasions, being careful to choose muted colors so they don't upstage their royal companions. Ladies of the Bedchamber are drawn from the aristocracy and have titles of their own.

**Lord Chamberlain:** The Lord Chamberlain oversees the royal household and is responsible for ceremonial occasions.

**Master of the Household:** The Master of the Household is responsible for the domestic arrangements at royal residences and for preparing the Court Circular, a daily listing of the official events royals will be attending.

**Mistress of the Robes:** The Mistress of the Robes is a senior lady-in-waiting.

**Pages:** Pages are senior in rank to footmen and under-butlers. For everyday, they wear blue coats and waistcoats and black trousers. For special occasions, they wear black-and-gold coats, white breeches and stockings and black pumps.

**Palace Housekeeper:** The palace housekeeper is responsible for all the female domestic staff and the royal linens and laundry.

**Palace Steward:** The palace steward is responsible for all the male domestic staff, including pages, footmen, under-butlers, and yeomen. He also looks after the royal catering arrangements.

**Press Secretary:** The press secretary keeps the balance between publicizing permitted facts and protecting royal mystery.

**Private Secretary:** Private secretaries are the channels of communication between the royal family and the government. They look after the royals' official programs and official correspondence. They also make sure royals don't make statements or send out letters that might get them into trouble. They come with assistant private secretaries because the royals are so busy.

**Under-Butlers:** Under-butlers are general assistants to more senior members of the household, such as yeomen.

**Women of the Bedchamber:** Women of the Bedchamber are ladies-in-waiting who wait on the Queen privately. They run personal errands for her and deal with her correspondence.

**Yeoman:** There are a number of different kinds of yeomen: Yeoman of the Guard, Yeomen of the Gold and Silver, Yeomen of the Glass and China Pantries, and the Traveling Yeoman (who looks after the royal luggage). The main thing is that the yeomen are all guarding something, whether it is the sovereign or the sovereign's possessions. The Yeomen of the Guard used to protect the sovereign, especially in battle. Today, their role is mostly ceremonial. To make sure they look suitably venerable and impressive in their starched scarlet uniforms, all Yeomen of the Guard must be over fifty and over 180 cm (5 feet 10 inches) tall.

children when he and his wife, Princess Diana, separated. Prince Andrew also kept Ms. Anderson in his thoughts after he became an adult. When he and his wife, Sarah Ferguson, realized they were going to have to announce the end of their marriage, Andrew was worried. "What shall we say to Mabel?" he asked.

Throughout the ups and downs of their young lives, William and Harry often turned to their personal protection officers for encouragement and support. When William was five, his bodyguards helped him catch toads in a pond, and they were always ready to play a pick-up game of soccer if there were idle moments to fill. Both boys burst into tears when Prince Charles would not let Harry invite his personal protection officer, Sgt. David Sharp, to one of his birthday parties. The officer was subsequently moved to other duties because Charles was worried that Harry was getting too emotionally attached to him.

In Britain, it is considered important to maintain a respectful difference between royals and people of lower status. Observing royal etiquette is one way of achieving this. If you are a British royal, you will observe a lot of bowing and curtsying on your royal walkabouts. When a royal approaches, people of lesser rank (which is just about everybody!) are expected to bow or curtsy as a sign of respect. People who think they are likely to meet royals often spend hours practicing their curtsies or bows, but despite the preparation they don't always get it right. Sometimes men get flustered and curtsy instead of bowing (especially if they are with their wives). Some people curtsy or bow too low and topple over. (You, as a young royal, must maintain a proper sense of decorum and hide the urge to laugh at these mishaps.) Many European courts have done away with curtsies and bows, considering them to be outdated. Even the British queen has conceded that some people have either given up this custom or simply don't know what they are supposed to do. But she still appreciates curtsies and bows from those who are knowledgeable about royal etiquette.

Royal etiquette extends to physical contact as well. If you are royal, no one may touch you except if you offer to shake their hand. An official at the 2000 Olympics in Sydney, Australia, accidentally touched Princess Anne when escorting her to the hockey stadium and had to apologize. And when the former Australian prime minister Paul Keating touched the Queen at a reception at Parliament House in 1992, the press immediately dubbed him "The Lizard of Oz."

As a young royal, you will find that there are lots of older royals who outrank you, so you'll need to apply yourself to learning the proper etiquette too. The rules may seem strict, but they are more relaxed than they used to be. When King Henry VIII was a boy in the fifteenth century, he had to go down on one knee every time his father spoke to him. When George VI first became king in 1936, his two daughters, the princesses Elizabeth and Margaret, were expected to curtsy to him, but this was considered impractical and the requirement was dropped. When Elizabeth succeeded her father, she let her children off the hook on this one as well, but they still observed proper etiquette with older members of the royal family. Before he was three, Charles learned to bow before offering his cheek for a fleeting kiss from his great-grandmother, Queen Mary. He also knew he was not to sit down in the presence of his grandfather, King George VI, until he was invited to do so.

With all this deferential behavior going on, it would be perfectly natural if you, as a young royal, started to throw your weight around a bit to see how other people would react. Both Princess Elizabeth and later her daughter, Princess Anne, discovered to their great delight that they could make the palace sentries snap to attention just by walking back and forth in front of them. Prince Andrew took this delightful game one step further by tying together the laces on the sentries' boots. While on duty the sentries couldn't look down, so there was nothing they could do about it. (Sentries assigned to guard Buckingham Palace must have a great deal of patience when there are young royals in residence.)

The young Prince William thought birthday parties were a good place to exercise some royal clout. On more than one occasion he was overheard to say, "When I am king, I'm going to make a new rule that …" And once, when he wasn't allowed to blow out the candles on someone else's cake, he shouted, "When I'm king, I'll order my knights to come and chop your head off!" (He obviously hadn't yet learned about the restricted powers of a constitutional monarch. Queen Victoria, his great-great-great-great-grandmother, never quite got the hang of the restrictions, either, and was constantly having run-ins with her government ministers.) Weddings provided a good opportunity for issuing orders too. At the age of six, at the wedding of Princess Diana's cousin Edward Barry, Prince William took it upon himself to organize the other five pageboys and the four bridesmaids (that's flower girls if you live in North America) outside the church. "Get back! Get in line!" he commanded the group of tiny attendants.

In his royal bossiness, Prince William seems to have been following in his grandmother's footsteps. Princess Elizabeth was once overheard ordering a young visitor to "Curtsy, girl!" On another occasion, she tugged on an adult's sleeve and commanded the adult to listen by saying, "Royalty speaking!" These days, however, bossiness doesn't go down well, even if you are a royal. William once tried to order the soldiers in the Royal Highland Fusiliers Regiment around, and when they didn't do as he said, he threatened to sack the lot of them. The soldiers complained that he was becoming a "cocky little brat."

## Good Manners

Queen Elizabeth's younger sister, Princess Margaret, was a very well-mannered little girl. One day J.M. Barrie, the author of *Peter Pan*, came to tea at the Queen Mother's ancestral home in Scotland, Glamis Castle. He was seated next to Princess Margaret, and between their place settings there was a brightly wrapped Christmas cracker. When he asked her whose it was, Princess Margaret solemnly replied, "It's yours *and* mine."

If you're going to be good at being royal, you must deal with your position in life with grace, and your training for this begins in your early years (although you will undoubtedly slip up once or twice along the way). Prince Charles felt the most important thing for his children was manners: "If they turn out to be not very bright or very qualified, at least if they have reasonable manners, they will get so much further in life than if they did not have any at all."

Queen Elizabeth the Queen Mother was one young lady who never had any trouble being gracious. Although she married into the royal family rather than being born royal, her innate good manners are one reason she made such a popular queen. Nine-year-old Elizabeth Bowes-Lyons, as she was then, was a precociously well-mannered child. When Miss Goff, the headmistress of her school, called at Elizabeth's home to give her weekly progress report to Elizabeth's mother, Lady Strathmore was late. Elizabeth had the butler take Miss Goff's coat and sat her down by the fire in the sitting room. "I know it is rather early, but I do think fires so cheer up a room, don't you?" she said to put her guest at ease. She then pulled the bell to order tea and instructed the maid to tell cook to put plenty of cream on the scones.

Her mother had still not shown up by the time the tea arrived. As Elizabeth poured, she ventured, "Well, Miss Goff, as Mama appears to be unduly delayed, for which I am sure she is so very sorry, perhaps you should tell *me* about my progress. And please don't hesitate to include any shortcomings requiring correction." Indeed, Elizabeth had been well mannered for years before that incident. When she was only four years old, she met one of the servants at Glamis Castle, her home in Scotland, with the following carefully worded greeting: "How do you do, Mr. Ralston. I haven't seen you look so well for years and years."

Not every child exhibits such natural skills in royal politeness, though. William's parents lost no time in trying to mold their little "thug" into a proper gentleman. By the age of three, he had learned to wave every time he saw a crowd. And although he still stuck his tongue out from time to time, especially at the media, he engaged in this behavior less and less often.

(William learned how to stick out his tongue at the press from his cousin, Peter Phillips. As soon as he discovered this was not acceptable royal behavior, he was quick to pass his newfound knowledge on to his younger brother, Harry. When Harry stuck his tongue out at photographers, William said: "Stop it, Harry. That's very naughty.")

By the age of four, William had perfected the Windsor wave (arm held up with a bent elbow, hand rotating slightly from the wrist). He had learned how to give the royal handshake, and his mother, Princess Diana, began to push him forward in crowds. He also got into the habit of saying lots of pleases and thank-yous. (His father, Prince Charles, was very polite as a boy. Charles even used to say please when asking his dog to perform tricks.)

## Bad Habits

Like any children, royal children in training are affected by the behavior of the adults around them. The problem for royal child-minders is that these adults are often people who hold high public office, which can make royal training diffi-cult. When they were young, both Princess Elizabeth and Princess Margaret bit their nails. Their governess, Crawfie, was trying hard to get them to stop when one day the little princesses observed the British prime minister, Neville Chamberlain, giving his nails a good chew. The girls were quick to point out that if the prime minister was allowed to bite his nails, they didn't see why they should have to stop biting theirs.

At age five, William stood at his mother's side and shook hands with 180 dignitaries at a reception for international fashion writers at his home, Kensington Palace. He also began to open doors for women and started calling men "Sir." (Royals are nothing if not traditional.)

As William grew older, he learned to make small talk with strangers after holiday church services near the royal family estates of Sandringham and Balmoral. He would say such things as "Where do you come from?" Whatever the answer, he would reply with that favorite royal standby: "How interesting."

By the age of nine, William was getting to be a pro. On St. David's Day, March 1, 1992, he worked a crowd of 2,500, shaking hands firmly and smiling broadly. The setting was Cardiff, Wales, and William was sporting a yellow daffodil in honor of St. David, the country's patron saint. Only once did he inquire how long all the hand-shaking was going to last, and then only because his mother asked him how he was doing.

At ten, William was seen offering his arm to steady Queen Elizabeth the Queen Mother as she left church, holding an umbrella over her head to shield her from the rain. He was a perfect little gentleman escorting an exceedingly well-mannered old lady.

Unfortunately, good manners alone will not be enough to get you through the grueling round of royal duties you will be expected to perform when you are older. There are all kinds of other skills you'll need to acquire. One of these is to eat what is put on your plate, whether you're used to eating it or not. When you are on an official tour, royal advisors scout out a territory beforehand and make a list of foods you should not be served. When Queen Elizabeth made a visit to Italy in 2000, her list included garlic (because she'd have to meet a lot of people and didn't want smelly breath), spaghetti (because it's too messy), and spicy foods (in case they did not agree with her). No one, it seems, had thought to put goat on the list (which the Queen usually sees in Britain only in the form of regimental mascots). The Italians rose to the occasion. They served the Queen succulent young goat in a chestnut sauce. The Queen, seasoned professional that she is, calmly ate what was put before her.

(William will likely have no difficulty eating what is put before him either, since when he was young he enjoyed Marmite sandwiches.

Those of you not acquainted with this British delicacy might like to rush out and buy yourself a jar, just to see if you have what it takes to be a royal. Some people unused to this dark, salty spread have suggested that they would rather eat road tar.)

Another useful royal skill is not getting bored easily. It is said that the grandmother of the last German kaiser was the only member of the Prussian court who was not bored out of her mind at official receptions. Her secret was the daily walks she used to take when she was young — she had been taught to address a few well-chosen remarks to every tree she passed. Even the most boring people are usually more interesting conversationalists than trees, so she considered herself well prepared for life at court. Being a good actor — or taking a genuine delight in the task at hand — can also help. When Queen Elizabeth the Queen Mother was queen, she perfected the art of sailing merrily through royal ceremonial occasions. She managed to make it look as though there was nothing in the world she would rather be doing than laying a foundation stone or making a speech.

Of course, it takes practice to master the art of the royal occasion. The first time out, most young royals fall short of the mark. During his mother's long and (to him) tedious coronation ceremony — it did last over three hours and he was just four years old — Charles kept running his hands through his hair and sniffing them. It turned out he was trying to discover what strange cream his nanny had used to tame his recently trimmed hair. When four-year-old William got bored at his uncle Andrew's wedding, he passed the time by pulling faces at the little girls who were presenting flowers to the Queen. Then he stuck his tongue out at six-year-old Laura Fellowes when she wouldn't join in his games. Photographers caught his antics on film and the pictures appeared in newspapers the next day.

William certainly wasn't the first young royal to find family weddings tedious. In 1863, three-year-old Prince William of Prussia (later Kaiser Wilhelm II of Germany, the leader who started the First World War) had a really bad day at the wedding of his uncle Edward, Prince of Wales, to Princess Alexandra of Denmark. First William threw things: a muff from a carriage window, the stone from his ceremonial dagger across the chapel floor at Windsor. Then he pretended he was sick, because he didn't want to leave the toy donkey he was playing with in the castle corridor. When two of his uncles finally dragged him off, Prince William whiled away the time at the wedding ceremony by biting them.

Even slightly older royals sometimes have problems if left to their own devices. When George V was crowned, five of his children — David, Bertie, Mary, Harry, and Little George — rode together unaccompanied in an open carriage. On the way to the coronation ceremony, all went well. The little princes and princess waved graciously as the crowds cheered. On the way back, however, it was a different story. Bertie and Harry decided they needed more room and tried to stuff Little George under the seat. Mary first ignored them and then dove in to separate the three boys, losing her coronet in the scuffle. Eventually, she managed to both find her coronet and pry her brothers apart, and the children were much better behaved for the rest of the journey.

As a royal adult, you will need to remain cool, calm, and collected even when it seems that disaster is certain to strike. There were many heart-stopping moments during King George VI's coronation. First the Dean of Westminster, who was responsible for dressing the king in the white surplice that was to go under his coronation robes, tried to put the garment on the king inside out. Then the Archbishop of Canterbury had his thumb over some words the king was supposed to read out loud, and the Lord Great Chamberlain couldn't do up the belt buckle on the king's sword belt, so the king had to do it up himself. As if that wasn't enough, the people who were putting the crown on the king's head weren't sure which way round it was supposed to go, and they twisted it in a number of different directions while they were trying to decide. Finally, the king nearly fell over when a bishop stepped on his robe. Understandably a bit cranky by then, the king lost no time in telling the bishop to get off.

Queen Elizabeth II had her own moment of panic at her coronation in 1953. The red carpet in Westminster Abbey had been laid with the pile facing the wrong way. When Queen Elizabeth tried to walk down the aisle, the gold fringe of her robes caught on the carpet and held her back. "Get me started!" she hissed in dismay to the Archbishop of Canterbury. At least she didn't have her father's problems with the crown: two small stars had been applied to mark the front.

If you are easily embarrassed (or just plain clumsy), then maybe being a royal is not for you. In 1984, while visiting President Kaunda in Zambia, Prince Charles had an embarrassing encounter with a lionskin rug. He noted in his diary: "I put my foot in the mouth of a large lion which was pretending to be a carpet in the Hall." You'd think he would have avoided the lion after that, but, no: the next day he reported that the lion had managed to ambush him once again!

(It is likely, though, that not all the jokes will be at your expense. Sometimes it is the mishaps of the guests that provide amusement for the royals. When Hugh Scanlon of the Trades Union Congress was lunching with Queen Elizabeth, he dropped a bit of roast potato on the floor. He fervently hoped that no one would notice, but no such luck. A royal corgi came by, sniffed the potato, and decided to give it a miss. "It's not your day, is it?" observed the Queen.)

As a royal, you'll also have to get over worrying about what your friends might think of you. An ancestor of Prince William's, the future King Edward VIII, took one look at the clothes he was supposed to wear for the ceremony presenting him as the Prince of Wales and had a temper tantrum. He said all his friends in the navy would laugh at him. His mother, Queen Mary, eventually persuaded him to get dressed up in the white satin breeches and purple velvet surcoat edged with ermine. (An ermine is a member of the weasel family whose coat turns white in winter. White ermine is a favorite choice for trimming royal robes.)

Even if you don't mind the look of the royal wardrobe, the clothes are often uncomfortable to wear. King George V nearly fainted when he had to wear his heavy coronation robes in a ceremony in India in 1911. According to Prince Charles, the ceremonial outfit for Knights of the Garter also presents some problems. The Order of the Garter is awarded as a sign of royal favor. A recipient (known as a knight) dresses up in blue velvet robes and a black velvet hat with a big, fluffy white feather. He or she also wears a blue garter just below the left knee. Prince Charles reported that the stockings worn to display this honor were "boiling to wear and come up to one's thighs — a crazy outfit really, but the only way (as yet) to wear the true garter."

The main function of royal clothes is to set yourself apart from your subjects and to lend ceremony to important occasions. Queen Elizabeth the Queen Mother was always ready to dress properly if the occasion demanded it. On a tour of South Africa with her husband,

King George VI, she put on full evening dress and jewels at ten o'clock in the morning to meet with an assembly of Zulu chiefs, because she knew this was what people expected of a queen. In 1939, she and George VI were traveling across Canada by train. Along the way, a group of farmers who had trekked some distance hoping to get a glimpse of the royal couple were not disappointed. The queen arose in the middle of the night and put on a warm dressing gown and her best tiara so that she could go out on the observation deck and wave to them.

The royal importance of dressing correctly for every occasion caused great consternation on one occasion during the Second World War. The young princesses, Elizabeth and Margaret, had been sent to the relative safety of Windsor Castle while their parents stayed behind at Buckingham Palace. One night the air-raid siren at Windsor sounded. Everyone was supposed to go to the bomb shelter in the basement, but the princesses' governess, Crawfie, waited in vain for their nurse, Alah, to bring the girls down. When there was still no sign of them, Crawfie rushed up to the nursery. The prim and proper Alah was making sure that the princesses were suitably attired before they left the room. The next time, Alah was told sternly, the girls were to throw their coats on over their nightclothes and get moving.

So: as a young royal you must learn to dress correctly for ceremonial occasions (but recognize when personal safety is more important than clothes!), stifle yawns during long presentations, eat what's put in front of you, mind your manners at all times, and keep calm even when things are going horribly wrong. Your preparation for royal life is the ultimate in on-the-job training, and you might want to follow Prince Charles's advice. He said, "I learnt the way a monkey learns — by watching its parents."

# FOUR

# Behind Castle Doors

AS A ROYAL you will likely have a selection of lovely castles and palaces that you can live in or visit. A castle is a large fortified building, often with battlements and towers, and — if you are lucky — perhaps even a drawbridge. (His Serene Highness Prince Hans-Adam II of Liechtenstein has an electronically operated drawbridge at the castle where he lives.) But castles are often drafty and inconvenient, and by the seventeenth century, many European sovereigns wanted to move into elegant palaces where they could throw huge parties to impress people with the dazzling court life.

The palace of Versailles outside Paris, France, has been called the greatest palace in Europe. It became the permanent seat of the French king Louis XIV's court and government in 1678. The palace itself covered 10 hectares (25 acres), and in the section known as the Grand Commun, 1,500 high functionaries of the court lived and worked. The stables were so magnificent that a prince of Hanover once said that he was not as well housed as the king of France's horses. The 100 hectares (250 acres) of grounds were filled with formal gardens, fountains, and wooded areas where before there had been nothing but barren landscape.

Such gorgeous palaces are all well and good if you want to live all your life on show — as Louis XIV was happy to do — but if you want a more comfortable private life and functional offices, palaces are too large and the design of their rooms is not practical. Over the next couple of hundred years, monarchs who had inherited huge palaces remodeled them, creating smaller living apartments and places to work. Then, in the twentieth century, European monarchs began to abandon their palaces altogether, turning them into museums and using them officially for state occasions only. For instance, the Royal Palace in Madrid, which was started in 1738 and took nearly thirty years to complete, was abandoned as a royal residence in 1931. Today, the Spanish royal family lives in Zarzuela Palace. Although it is a few hundred years old, it is more like a large country house than a palace, and it has been fitted with all modern conveniences.

The British queen is not yet ready to abandon Buckingham Palace, which was originally built as a grand private residence in the early 1700s. The palace is one of a number of state-owned royal houses where the British family may live and work. Others include Kensington Palace, St. James's Palace, and Clarence House in London, and Windsor Castle just outside London. The Queen privately owns Balmoral Castle in Scotland and Sandringham House in Norfolk.

Buckingham Palace is one of the best recognized landmarks in London after Big Ben — the imposing clock tower at the Houses of Parliament — and the Tower of London, where the famous Crown Jewels are now on display. Although it has been a royal residence since George III bought it for his queen, Charlotte, in 1761, the first sovereign to live there was Queen Victoria, who moved into the palace in 1837. Situated at the end of St. James's Park, Buckingham Palace is a regular stop for tourists, who come to watch the colorful ceremony that marks the official changing of the palace guards. (The forty-five-minute ceremony takes place at 11:30 each morning from April to June in the forecourt of the palace and every other day for the rest of the year.) Tourists also come to see if they can catch a glimpse of Queen Elizabeth. If the Royal Standard (a special royal flag) is flying from the palace flagpole, it means that the Queen is at home.

## Tea-Tray Toboggans

Althorp, the ancestral home of the Spencer family, where Princess Diana grew up, is larger than any of the royal residences other than Buckingham Palace. When William and Harry were young, Diana's brother, the Earl of Spencer, used to let them toboggan down the huge staircases at Althorp using tea trays.

Buckingham Palace was renovated and added on to by successive sovereigns, and today it is forty times larger than the original house. It has about 600 rooms (even the royal family seems a bit vague on how many rooms there are). It is so large that when Prince Charles's former governess, Miss Peebles, died there in 1968 (she was living out her retirement somewhere in the palace), it was two days before anyone noticed she was missing. Because of its long corridors and dark rooms, many residents find Buckingham Palace gloomy. But royal children appreciate the long corridors, which are good for playing soccer. Prince Charles's younger brother Andrew remembers smashing the odd pane of glass or two while kicking a ball about, but says he doesn't

Prince William and his younger brother, Prince Harry, are second and third in line to the British throne after their father, Prince Charles. In these photos, it is clear that they aren't worrying too much about what life holds in store for them. Five-year-old William (top) plays on his great-grandfather's personal fire engine at the royal estate at Sandringham, while three-year-old Harry sneaks a peek at the crowd waiting to see his grandmother Queen Elizabeth II's official birthday celebrations at Buckingham Palace in London.

As Prince William and Prince Harry got older, they had to put in royal appearances, such as this one in Canada in 1991. Here nine-year-old William and seven-year-old Harry put their royal training to good use as they shake hands with members of the public outside St. James's Church in Toronto.

Princess Diana did what she could to help Prince William and Prince Harry experience life as other young people do. In 1991, she took Harry on this splashy ride at Thorpe Park in Kent (right). They even lined up for their turn, just like everyone else. But despite these excursions, there's no hiding the fact these boys lead privileged lives. In the bottom photo, thirteen-year-old Harry gets to meet Baby Spice and the other Spice Girls after a concert in South Africa in 1997.

Traditionally, royal parents have spent more of their time seeing to their royal duties than bringing up their children. William and Harry's mother, Princess Diana, was determined to change this. The boys enjoyed a warm, loving relationship with her until she was tragically killed in a car accident in 1997.

These days one of the challenges of being royal is that the media tracks your every move. It's never too soon to start the royal training: at this official photo shoot for Prince William's second birthday, his father, Prince Charles, warned him that cameras and microphones would follow him for the rest of his life.

Balmoral, in Scotland, is the British royal family's favorite place to relax. Here they shoot, fish, and take long walks on the heather. It's often cold and wet, but this photo opportunity for the press seems to have been arranged on a particularly lovely day.

On April 15, 1999, sixteen-year-old Prince William became godfather to Prince Konstantine Alexios of Greece. The Greek royal family was forced into exile in 1967 and now lives in London. This tiny prince has seven godparents in all, four of them heirs to their country's thrones: Prince William of Britain (after his father, Prince Charles), Crown Prince Frederik of Denmark, Crown Princess Victoria of Sweden, and Prince Felipe of Spain. (William's arm is in a sling because he's just had an operation on his index finger, which was fractured in a rugby game.)

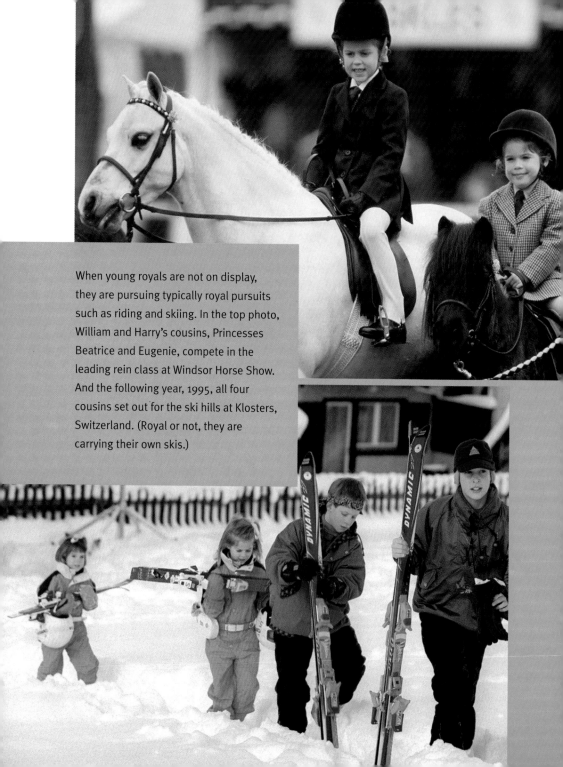

When young royals are not on display, they are pursuing typically royal pursuits such as riding and skiing. In the top photo, William and Harry's cousins, Princesses Beatrice and Eugenie, compete in the leading rein class at Windsor Horse Show. And the following year, 1995, all four cousins set out for the ski hills at Klosters, Switzerland. (Royal or not, they are carrying their own skis.)

remember breaking anything valuable. For adults, the corridors are often less alluring. Some have remarked that it seems to take the whole morning to get from one end of the palace to the other; others complain that food gets cold on its way from the palace kitchens to remote dining rooms.

Queen Elizabeth views Buckingham Palace as her "office." It has its own squash courts and post office in the basement, as well as a bombproof police station, a fallout shelter, and a swimming pool. The post office has a fluoroscope — a kind of x-ray machine — to check all incoming mail for hidden explosives. The office processes over 100,000 pieces of royal mail a year.

## Royal Mail

One of the perks of being royal is having your picture on the stamps you use. In 2000, the Royal Mail in Britain put Prince William on the 27p stamp they released in honor of his grandmother the Queen Mother's hundredth birthday. (Twenty-seven pence is about forty cents.) For William's eighteenth birthday, also in 2000, postal services in Ascension Island, British Virgin Islands, Cayman Islands, Falkland Islands, Fiji, South Georgia and South Sandwich Islands, and Tristan da Cunha — all of which have ties to Britain — released stamps showing William running alongside his pony, making his way to school, and waving at adoring crowds.

If you were born into the imperial family of Japan, however, your likeness would not appear on stamps. In Japan, it was thought that the sovereigns were descended from gods, and it was not considered fitting to display their images in such a common and commercial form.

Kensington Palace is the London home of the Queen's sister, Princess Margaret. It houses the families of the Duke and Duchess of Gloucester and of Prince and Princess Michael of Kent. It also contains a number of other "grace and favor" apartments, provided free for life to royal relations or people who have served the royal family. Prince Charles had an apartment in the palace from the time of his marriage in 1981 until Princess Diana's death in 1997, and Kensington Palace is one of the houses in which Prince William and Prince Harry grew up. (Charles once called Kensington Palace "the aunt heap" because so many royal relations lived there.)

St. James's Palace, across the park from Buckingham Palace, is now Prince Charles's London home. When William and Harry moved out of Kensington Palace after their mother's death, they moved into York House, a five-bedroom home within St. James's Palace. William has his own private apartment at the top of York House with a big television and lots of CDs. If he invites friends over and they want to spend the night, they have to stretch out on the sitting room floor, as there are only three rooms in the apartment: a sitting room, a bedroom, and a bathroom.

Clarence House, which adjoins St. James's Palace, served as a royal home until 1942 when the Duke of Connaught died and the house fell vacant. Since the Second World War had broken out, Clarence House was used as the headquarters for the Red Cross Society and the St. John Ambulance Association and Brigade for the next four years. In 1948, the house was renovated for Princess Elizabeth and her husband, Prince Philip. Prince Charles was on the way, and the young couple wanted to move from Buckingham Palace into a home of their own. They lived in Clarence House until they moved back to Buckingham Palace when

Elizabeth became queen. Clarence House is now home to the Queen Mother when she is in London.

Royal Lodge in Windsor Great Park is the Queen Mother's country residence. When King George V offered the lodge to her and her husband in 1931, it had been mostly unoccupied for nearly a hundred years. On weekends the young couple would gather up their daughters, the princesses Elizabeth and Margaret, and escape their London home in Piccadilly to tame the wilderness around the lodge. Whoever else might be there — secretary, duke, valet, or weekend guest — was usually handed an ax or saw to help hack away at the undergrowth. One time, a huge Guards officer spent the weekend breaking in his new bearskin — the tall furry hat worn by the sentries at Buckingham Palace — while maneuvering a wheelbarrow around the grounds.

The place where the Queen likes to spend her weekends is also located in Windsor Great Park. Windsor Castle is the largest inhabited castle in the world. It has been a royal home for over 900 years. The royal nursery at Windsor has four separate rooms where children can play and sleep, a kitchen, and two bathrooms. But if you were to stay at Windsor as a royal baby today, you would not sleep in the nursery. Your side of the royal family would be assigned a tower all to yourselves, and you and your nanny would get together with the children from the other towers in the nursery for meals.

Windsor is the Queen's weekend retreat. It is just a few minutes away from Eton, which is where William and Harry went to school in their teens, so it was easy for them to stop by for tea with their grandmother on Sunday afternoons. (As she is queen, they couldn't drop in unannounced but had to be sure to make an appointment first.)

All members of the royal family own private estates in the country where they can entertain their friends, and relax and pursue their hobbies and interests. Charles's country home is called Highgrove. Here he has a walled garden, a work-in-progress of which he is very proud, and an organic farm. His sister, Princess Anne, lives at Gatcombe Park in Gloucestershire. Her 200-hectare (500-acre) estate includes a farm and an internationally acclaimed equestrian center run by the princess's first husband, Mark Phillips. This makes it convenient for Anne's children, Peter and Zara, to divide their time between the two parents.

The British royal family is especially fond of the two estates Queen Elizabeth owns privately: Balmoral and Sandringham. These are places where the whole family can go to relax, and where friends and official guests are invited to enjoy the British countryside.

Balmoral is the royal family's holiday home in the Scottish Highlands. Surrounded by rugged peaks, this thirty-bedroom Victorian castle is situated on a 20,000-hectare (50,000-acre) estate in a valley eighty kilometers (fifty miles) southwest of Aberdeen. Visitors enjoy bracing temperatures and lots of fresh air. Reporters are banned, so it is a haven of tranquility after a season of royal appointments. The Queen Mother has two houses in Scotland: Birkall on the Balmoral estate and the Castle of Mey on the far-off Caithness coast near John O'Groats, the most northerly point on the British mainland.

The British royal family is mostly passionate about Balmoral. "I miss the mountains deeply and the noisy silence of Deeside," Prince Charles wrote in a letter from Cambridge University. "He loves being out on the hill with his gun and his dog," Sarah Ferguson said of her husband, Prince Andrew. She added, "[At Balmoral,] he became easy and full of gentle fun, his truest self. It was lovely to see." Princess Diana once reported, "William is at his happiest at Balmoral." But the place is not to everyone's taste. Edward VII called the castle "a Highland barn with a thousand drafts," and Princess Diana didn't like it much either. One time she left Prince Charles there with just two parting words: "Boring. Raining."

In order to enjoy Balmoral, you must have a high tolerance for being wet and cold. (In fact, this is pretty much a requirement for being a member of the British royal family, given Britain's climate and the draftiness of even the most luxurious of royal residences.) Neither Queen Elizabeth nor her mother seems to notice the cold much. When she is out in the country, there is nothing the Queen likes better than to pull on a pair of rubber boats and an anorak, tie her scarf under her chin, and take her dogs out for a nice long walk, or to have a groom saddle up one of her horses so she can ride around the royal estate. As long as it is not freezing cold or pelting down with rain, the Queen and her children are always up for a family barbecue or a picnic outside when the royal family is on holiday.

When the royal family spends time at Balmoral, royal horses and hunting dogs are driven up from Sandringham so there will be horses for everyone to ride and plenty of dogs to collect the birds that fall victim to the royal shooting parties. You'll know right away when you arrive at the castle that the family who lives here loves the outdoor life. The hallway is crammed full of dog dishes, fishing rods, and rain gear. You'll also see that this is a family that values outdoor pursuits over indoor comforts, for the plumbing in the castle is rather ancient and conversations held in bedrooms can travel down the pipes.

If you're a young British royal weekending at Balmoral Castle when there are guests, you will likely be woken by the stirring sound of bagpipes being played under your bedroom window at 9:00 a.m. sharp. (It may not be your idea of an ideal way to start the day, but this is what the Queen likes.) Prince Philip will already be gone, having led the adult male guests out onto the moor at 8:45 to shoot grouse or stalk Highland stags (male deer).

If they are going stalking, they'll have taken their lunches carefully wrapped in small waterproof bags. They'll have buns filled with meat, mutton pies, plum pudding, ginger beer or lager, and perhaps a small hip flask of whisky to keep out the cold. Deer are shy animals, and to get close enough to shoot one in the Highlands, where there is very little cover, you have to lie down in soggy heather and inch your way forward on your stomach — through icy streams if necessary — until you have one lined up for the perfect shot. That's the reason for the waterproof lunch and a nip of something to stave off the cold.

While the men are out tramping the moors with their guns, the Queen will have breakfast in bed and then go for a ride on one of her horses at 10:00. Bodyguards on mountain bikes will accompany her. As a young royal, you're welcome to join her on your pony if you like. If you don't want to ride, you can go for a hike or take out one of the ancient bicycles kept in the castle hallway. (Even if you'd rather stay inside, you're expected to get out for at least some sort of exercise in the fresh air.)

If Prince Philip and the other men have gone shooting rather than stalking, they won't have taken their lunches with them, and you and the other guests will be expected to meet them for a picnic on the heather after the morning's activities. Family members and guests are driven out to the picnic in Land Rovers. The food arrives in a van specially outfitted (according to a design by Prince Philip) to keep hot food hot and cold food cold. The picnic hampers contain everything you need for a picnic: white linen, silver cutlery, and menu cards.

The afternoon is spent tramping the moors to pick up dead birds or fishing for salmon in the River Dee until teatime. You'll have to watch out, though. Even though the media is banned from Balmoral, photographers sometimes intrude. William once told his little brother, who wanted to play down by the river after their morning ride, "You mustn't go down there, Harry. The press are there and they mustn't see you." On another occasion, Prince Charles had been stalking a stag for a week. He finally had the animal in his sights when a photographer popped up out of the bushes, scaring the stag away. The photographer did try to be helpful. "I think I've got a *picture* of the stag if that might be of any consolation to His Royal Highness?" he said.

After tea you can rest, and then you must get dressed in your finest for a formal dinner. Predinner drinks are served at 6:00, dinner promptly at 8:15. Don't be late, because it is extremely rude to arrive after the Queen. The table will be laid with lots of crystal and silver decorated with a thistle design dating from Queen Victoria's day. After dinner, the men will have port and cigars in one room while the women retire to chat in another. As a young royal, your Saturday evening's entertainment could be a private screening of a soon-to-be released movie, or it might be a wild game of hide-and-seek or kick-the-can up and down the palace corridors. Adults will often join in — including the prime minister, if he or she is up for the weekend. The Queen Mother likes to play bridge in the evenings if she can find partners, and solitaire if she cannot. Princess Margaret plays the piano, and she is always happy to entertain the party with songs and music until the early hours of the morning.

The Queen attends church on Sunday, and after lunch you can watch the guests leave with their clothes freshly laundered and neatly packed, their cars freshly scrubbed, and boxes of birds added to their luggage.

When the British royals are not at Balmoral, their next-favorite place to relax is Sandringham, their country estate in Norfolk. The house used to be much larger than it is today — a legacy from the days when Edward VII liked to throw lavish parties here — but in the 1970s, the Queen had a dilapidated wing that used to house servants' quarters demolished. Unfortunately, Sandringham is much less private than Balmoral, as there is a public footpath that runs right through the estate. (In Britain, public footpaths follow ancient rights of way and are no respecters of private property.) Sandringham House is close to a village, and the Queen sometimes takes advantage of this to visit the local shops. One day a fellow shopper looked at her intently and then remarked how much she resembled the Queen. Queen Elizabeth, a little taken aback, replied: "How very reassuring."

Queen Elizabeth has both stables and kennels at Sandringham, so horses and dogs are always available for riding and shooting parties. The estate also grows grain, beets, peas, beans, apples, and other fruit. Sandringham has long supplied a frozen-food packager with peas and the makers of a concentrated fruit syrup with blackcurrants. Moving with the times, the Queen has made the name Sandringham into a trademark and is now selling apple juice made from estate apples.

The entranceway to the house at Sandringham opens up into a spacious room filled with comfortable furniture of the sort that's inviting for a nap after a long day out in the fresh air. When King Edward VII spent time here, visitors used to be greeted by a stuffed gorilla in the hallway, a souvenir from one of the king's foreign tours.

The pattern of the days at Sandringham is basically the same as in Scotland, except that there are no bagpipes and the picnic lunches are served indoors, because shooting parties here are held during the winter months. In the evenings, the Queen likes to do jigsaw puzzles, the bigger and more complicated the better. She challenges herself by completing them without looking at the picture on the lid. As a young royal, you can help, but it would be tactful to let the Queen put in the last pieces herself. Once again, there will usually be some evening activity that everyone gets in on. When Charles and Anne were little, the Queen and Prince Philip, the Queen Mother, Princess Margaret, and Princess Marina (the wife of the Queen's uncle, the Duke of Kent) would all rush around shrieking loudly as they chased one another down corridors and around rooms in lively games of tag.

When Queen Elizabeth's children were growing up, the Queen and her close relations would arrive at Sandringham to celebrate the New Year after an enormous Christmas celebration for the extended family at Windsor Castle. (Windsor Castle was large enough to accommodate all manner of Windsors.) Then, in 1988, the Queen had Windsor rewired. She decided to move the family Christmas celebration to Sandringham and to restrict it to the immediate family because of the smaller premises. After a disastrous fire at Windsor in 1992, the Queen made the move a permanent one; since then Prince William and Prince Harry and their royal cousins have all congregated at Sandringham to celebrate Christmas.

One of the downsides to being a member of the royal family is the number of cards you have to sign at Christmastime. Each year, from October through early December, the royal family sends out hundreds of cards. Homemade cards for close friends are encouraged. Prince Charles, Princess Anne, and Princess Margaret all made their own Christmas cards when they were young. The Queen used to paint bells and holly on the ones she made when she was a girl.

Christmas is a time of gift giving, and the Queen gives more gifts than most. Not only does she buy gifts for members of her family, she also gives gifts to all 650 or so of her full-time staff. The head house-keeper makes the purchases on the Queen's behalf. The Queen then presents each gift personally, along with a royal handshake. The tradition of the British sovereign personally giving Christmas gifts to servants was started by Queen Victoria's daughter-in-law, Queen Alexandra, who was famously kind-hearted. One Christmas at Sandringham she learned that a footman was homesick, and even though he was going to get an official present later, she couldn't resist presenting him with a pair of gold cuff links right away to cheer him up. (Her husband, Edward VII, reportedly said it was just as well the Crown Jewels were safely in the Tower of London, or Queen Alexandra would have had them auctioned off for charity.)

Queen Elizabeth used to do her own Christmas shopping at Harrods, the huge London department store, early in the morning before the store opened to the public. This became too much of a security hazard, however, and now another store sends a truckload of possible presents to Buckingham Palace. The Queen can then have a leisurely after-dinner browse in the comfort of her own living room to make her Christmas gift selections. An equerry does most of

Prince Charles's Christmas shopping for him. Charles generally avoids shopping in stores, although he does sometimes shop for presents at country craft fairs.

## Christmas Party

Princess Diana's father, the late Earl of Spencer, used to hold a pre-Christmas party in early December at his home, Althorp, for his grandchildren and the children of his friends and members of his household. The earl would always invite an entertainer and someone who dressed up as Santa Claus. One of Prince William and Prince Harry's favorite entertainers was Ernie Almond, otherwise known as Smartie Artie, who would dress up in colorful costumes to do conjuring tricks and a ventriloquist act with his puppet, Scruffy. After the entertainment, there would be a huge tea. (It was important to keep an eye on Harry if chocolate cake was served, as he adored it and ate it rather messily.) After tea, the guests would open presents, all bought personally by the earl. About forty children attended these parties, and Mr. Almond said that attending the event was like "going into fairyland."

Two Christmas parties are held before Christmas at Buckingham Palace, one for staff and one for extended family. Attendance at the family party is mandatory, and the Queen decides whether there will be a traditional Christmas menu or something completely different. The Queen and Prince Philip then travel to Sandringham, to be joined by their immediate family no later than Christmas Eve. Away from London, the Queen works on her official Christmas broadcast to the nation, which is taped the week before Christmas to be televised on Christmas Day.

The British royal family has strongly influenced the way many people celebrate Christmas today. It was Queen Victoria's husband, Prince Albert, who introduced the German custom of a lighted Christmas tree to Britain. Prince Albert also came up with the idea of preprinted Christmas cards to cut down on the annual chore of sending out Christmas greetings. King George I, who reigned from 1714 to 1729, was responsible for the plum pudding — not everyone's favorite Christmas treat. To this day, each member of the Queen's household gets a Christmas pudding each year. The puddings used to be made in the palace kitchens. Today they are bought from the British grocery store Tesco.

The British royal family follows the European custom of opening their gifts on Christmas Eve. Although they are accustomed to receiving lavish gifts when they are on official tours or hosting events for visiting dignitaries, within the family they restrict themselves to modest, useful gifts. Nine-year-old Prince Charles wrote to his great-uncle Louis Mountbatten: "Do you think I could not have the silly-putty for my birthday but please can I have a bicycle if you can." His great-uncle agreed but said that, because the bicycle was an expensive present, it would have to do for Christmas as well. As a schoolboy, Charles was good with clay, and he used to make goofy animal mugs to give to family members. One year he gave his sister, Anne, a doormat, and Anne herself has been known to give people jars of homemade jam. When Prince William and Prince Harry were young, they were not given extra allowances to buy family Christmas presents, but were encouraged to continue the family tradition of homemade gifts. If they were lucky, they would receive more extravagant Christmas gifts from people outside their family: one year they received a beautiful rocking horse for the palace nursery.

After the royal family has opened all their presents, they go to midnight mass. On Christmas Day there is a huge lunch with turkey and Christmas pudding. (In 1851, roast turkey was substituted for the traditional royal roast swan.) After the Christmas lunch, the family sits down to watch the Queen's broadcast on television and then splits up to nap or walk off all the food. They meet again for tea (the Queen pours) and a formal dinner in the evening followed by games and dancing.

On Boxing Day, the day after Christmas, the family is up bright and early. (If you're not an early riser, perhaps this is not the family for you.) A hearty breakfast is served at 8:30 before the traditional Boxing Day shoot, which is organized by Prince Philip. After the shoot there is tea and then another huge dinner.

Huge castles and palaces are good for large family gatherings, but if they are very old, they sometimes accommodate more than just the living members of the family. If you are a young royal with a long family history, the castles and palaces you visit with your family may be visited by ghosts as well. Windsor Castle, the oldest British royal residence, claims the most ghosts these days. There are said to be at least twenty-five of them jostling for space in the castle at night. One of the oldest of these is Herne the Hunter. In the fourteenth century he was found dead in Windsor Great Park, hanging from an oak tree. In 1863, in an attempt to banish Herne's ghost, Queen Victoria had the old tree chopped down and burned the wood in the castle fireplaces. But Herne didn't want to leave. They say he can sometimes still be seen on misty nights riding over what are now the royal polo grounds. If you listen carefully, you can hear the baying of his hounds in the wind.

When author Hector Bolitho slept in one of the guest rooms at Windsor Castle, his bedroom door kept mysteriously opening and closing. In the end, he had to keep his walking stick by the bed so he could push the door shut if the ghost forgot to close it on its way out. Another guest caught a glimpse of this ghost in a mirror in the hallway. The shadowy shape disappeared when it reached the bottom of the stairs.

Not surprisingly, the ghosts of a number of former kings and queens are also said to be hanging around. A gouty old Henry VIII limps and moans around the cloisters. His daughter, Elizabeth I, prefers to spend her time in the library. She usually contents herself with frightening late-night readers with a swish of her skirts, leaving a lingering smell of rose water, her favorite fragrance. At the turn of the last century, the Empress Frederick of Germany was sure the ghostly figure she saw in the library was wearing a long nightgown. She could well have been right, as the library at Windsor was once Queen Elizabeth I's bedchamber.

The ghost of Queen Elizabeth I shares the library with that of Charles I, who was beheaded in 1649. (Apparently Charles's Windsor ghost still has his head on, though.) The library was also where King George III was confined in periods of madness in the early nineteenth century. The castle sentries used to salute the mad king whenever his bearded face appeared at a library window. Legend has it that one sentry dropped his rifle when he realized the king he was saluting had died four days before.

Buckingham Palace has a twentieth-century ghost — Major John Gwynne, a private secretary to King Edward VIII, who shot himself in his palace office in the early 1900s after becoming involved in a divorce scandal. And at Sandringham, the lively ghost of Dorothy Walpole, who died in the eighteenth century, thoroughly enjoys Christmas. She is reported to cause havoc in the servants' quarters, flinging Christmas cards about, stripping sheets from beds, and breathing heavily into people's ears. She once appeared to one of Prince Philip's Greek uncles as a reflection in a dressing-table mirror. Philip's uncle later recognized Walpole from a portrait he saw while visiting nearby Houghton Hall. Walpole had lived at Houghton Hall, where she obtained a divorce to escape her unhappy marriage.

At St. James's Palace, people say a lingering smell of blood is a reminder of the death of Sellis, valet to the Duke of Cumberland, who was found with his throat cut in 1810. The duke was acquitted of his servant's murder.

Gatcombe Park, Princess Anne's country house, is believed to be haunted by a huge black dog (a fitting specter for such a dog-loving family), the Hound of Odin, which accompanied the Vikings on their pillaging raids of the British countryside a thousand years ago.

Haunted or not, gloomy or much loved, royal residences are definitely a cut above the places most people call home. As a young royal, you will get used to dividing your time between palaces full of priceless antiques, with private secretaries bustling about to make sure all royal duties are fulfilled, and country retreats where you can relax, entertain your friends, and indulge in your favorite hobbies or pastimes.

# FIVE

# Royal Pursuits

SO WHAT KIND OF INTERESTS would it be useful for you to cultivate if you are thinking of becoming a member of a royal family? A love of animals would definitely be an asset. Many royals are very fond of animals. When you're dealing all day with adoring crowds and people you must be polite to, it must be refreshing to go home to a dog that wants nothing more than to flop down at your feet and have its tummy scratched. A love of sports and hunting and shooting would also be good. European royals are forever off on skiing or sailing holidays, or inviting other royals over for shooting parties on their country estates. They swim in their private pools, play tennis on their private courts, and often ride horses at a competitive level. (If you've been born into a position, instead of having to work for it, I guess it makes sense to want to prove yourself in other areas.) Enthusiasm for the outdoor life comes in handy if you end up doing some sort of military training, which is a definite possibility as most European sovereigns are also the head of their armed forces, so it's good to be acquainted with the military. Finally, if all this sounds rather too energetic for you, you could consider developing your artistic talents, as there are a few royals who prefer painting, photography, or theater to dashing around proving themselves on the sports field or shooting things.

If you're an animal lover, you'll fit right into the British royal family. Just about any animal will do. Three hundred years ago, King Charles II established a collection of exotic waterfowl in St. James's Park in London. Today the royal collection includes white-faced whistling ducks from the tropics, pelicans from Astrakhan and India, black swans from Australia, and red-beaked Cape teal from South Africa. And it's not just imported waterfowl that get special attention. Since medieval times, any swan in the British Isles that is not owned privately is the property of the sovereign. (The rule was introduced to stop just anyone from having swan for dinner; the birds were once a valuable source of fresh food during the cold winter months, and at one time they were in danger of being wiped out.) Today, even though the Queen doesn't expect any of them to become dinner, all the swans on the River Thames between Blackfriars and Henley are counted once a year. Those that belong to two ancient companies — the Dyers and the Vintners — are marked with notches in their beaks. All the rest are royal swans, which are left unmarked. This annual ceremony, known as Swan Upping, is performed by the Queen's official Swan Marker and his or her assistants, the Swan Uppers. Members of the swan-marking party are easy to spot as they wear scarlet jackets and travel in wooden rowboats flying colorful flags.

One of the most exotic animals owned by a British royal was the giraffe presented to Queen Victoria's uncle King George IV in 1827. Queen Victoria's son, Edward VII, and his wife, Queen Alexandra, continued the royal tradition of unusual pets with their menagerie at Sandringham House. Their collection included a miniature Indian pony called Nawab that the children used to ride right into the house. Queen

Alexandra didn't seem to mind. She recorded happily in her diary: "The dear little Indian pony came all the way upstairs into my dressing-room and walked down again."

## Man's Best Friend

Queen Victoria's great-grandfather, Frederic Lewis, Prince of Wales, had a dog whose collar read: "I am His Highness's dog at Kew. Pray tell me, sir, whose dog are you?"

There was also a black ram that Queen Alexandra saved from the cooking pot while she and King Edward VII were cruising on a boat down the Nile. The ram had been taken along to provide fresh meat during the journey. It broke free of its tether, trotted to where the queen was sitting, and laid its head on her knee. After such a display of affection, Alexandra couldn't bear the thought of the ram being eaten, and she had it shipped back to join her other animals in England. In keeping with his parents' collection of odd pets, George V owned a parrot called Charlotte, which used to walk about on the royal table at breakfast. As his wife, Queen Mary, was not as forgiving of animals in the house as his mother, Queen Alexandra, had been, the king would move the mustard pot to cover any messes the parrot made.

These days, with the exception of the children's zoo at the cream-colored palace in Amman where the four youngest children of the late King Hussein and Queen Noor of Jordan live, most royal families no longer have their own zoos. But the young British princes certainly have an interest in seeing animals in the wild.

Prince Harry is lucky to have been on two African safaris. When he was thirteen, his father, Prince Charles, took him and a school friend to Botswana. William was rather envious and said he, too, would like to see animals in Africa. He got his chance when both princes went on safari in South Africa just before William finished school at Eton. The princes slept in a tent at night, trekked through the bush on foot, and rode rivers in dugout canoes.

This is a big change from the kind of animal watching that British kings used to do. On his tours of Africa, Edward VII hunted crocodiles and elephants. When George V visited India in 1911, his hosts organized tiger shoots in his honor. One day, thirty-seven tigers were shot. Even Prince Philip shot a tiger while on a tour of India and Pakistan in 1961. He came in for considerable criticism as he was involved in setting up the World Wildlife Fund at the time — an organization he is still actively involved in.

Prince William is much more interested in conserving endangered wildlife than in bagging it for trophies. For his year off between school and university in 2000 and 2001, he made sure to include some adventure travel. First he joined a British army training exercise in the Central American country of Belize, where dense jungles are home to jaguars, pumas, ocelots, armadillos, tapirs, and crocodiles. Then he flew to the tropical paradise of Rodrigues Island, which is close to the second-largest barrier reef in the world. William snorkeled and did scuba diving in waters that are home to moray eels and great white, tiger, and mako sharks. Then it was off for a ten-week trip to Patagonia, where he spent some of his time radio-tracking rare southern Andean deer.

But although British royals no longer kill animals in foreign lands, they do still kill animals at home. This issue is very controversial. Lots of people oppose killing animals for sport, but others find nothing wrong with shooting animals such as deer or game birds, especially if you eat what you've killed or if animal or bird populations are getting out of hand and need to be controlled.

Shooting is a time-honored royal tradition in Britain. The first thing Edward VIII did when he became king was to set the clocks at Sandringham back half an hour to the correct time. His father, George V, had insisted on having them half an hour fast, so that he would be sure not to miss a moment's shooting. King George VI, Edward VIII's younger brother, loved shooting at Sandringham as much as his father did. The day the king died, he had been out shooting hares, and he had another shoot planned for the next day.

In a letter written in his early twenties, Charles thanked his great-uncle Louis Mountbatten for a shooting party. "The pheasants were carefully drilled to ensure the most exciting, indescribable, memorable, exhausting, record-breaking, finger-burning, shattering, thoroughly well-organised day," he wrote. As his sons grew up, Charles taught them both how to shoot Highland stags and introduced them to fox hunting.

Because they continue to hunt and shoot, members of the British royal family are constantly running up against animal welfare activists. There was a terrible fuss when Peter Phillips, Princess Anne's son, was caught on camera swinging a dead pheasant around his head. Queen Elizabeth came in for angry criticism in 2000, when she was spotted dispatching a not-quite-dead pheasant at Sandringham with an expert twist to its neck. Queen Elizabeth is an avid breeder of the working dogs used for royal shooting parties. She trains her Labradors and cocker spaniels to collect the downed birds. The spaniels go into deep brush to retrieve

## The Fruits of Royal Estates

Prince William and Prince Harry are lucky enough to have the Queen's country estates of Sandringham and Balmoral to visit when they want to unwind. Not only do these estates provide open spaces and country air, they also provide all manner of good country food. There is fresh venison from the deer hunts at both Sandringham and Balmoral, and fresh Scottish salmon from the waters of the River Dee. There are grouse (a small game bird) at Balmoral, pheasant and duck at Sandringham, and game fowl eggs from both estates. There are hazelnut and quince trees at Sandringham. When nutting season is over, the estate keepers squirrel the hazelnuts away in cloth bags buried underground, well out of the reach of frost. Stored in this manner, the nuts keep fresh for months. Prince Philip is fond of the hazelnuts; the Queen prefers the quince. A quince is a hard, applelike fruit. The trees at Sandringham produce enough fruit for a tangy royal quince jelly.

Down on the coastal mud flats, a salty sea-asparagus called samphire has been harvested since medieval times. Samphire from Sandringham was served at the wedding breakfast when Prince Charles and Princess Diana got married.

birds the larger Labs might miss. The Queen also enters her working dogs in competitions and, like any dog owner, is proud of them when they do well.

Prince William led his first pheasant shoot in 1995 and made the newspapers again when he felled his first stag at Balmoral with a single shot. William realized his actions would anger activists opposed to blood sports, and he advised his mother, Princess Diana, not to become the patron of an animal-rights charity. He told her: "Every time I kill [an animal], they'll blame you." Despite the adverse publicity it brings them, William and Harry keep up their hunting and shooting, including riding behind hounds that chase foxes across the British countryside.

Nearly all members of the British and many other European royal families learn to ride almost as soon as they can walk. When Queen Elizabeth the Queen Mother was young, she had a Shetland pony called Bob that used to follow her around like a dog. Queen Elizabeth got her first pony, Peggy, also a Shetland, when she was three. As a small girl, the Queen enjoyed taking care of toy horses in her nursery, real horses in her stables, and even imaginary horses in her head. When her longtime governess, Crawfie, first met the Queen (then Princess Elizabeth), she was sitting up in bed with a pair of toy reins in her hands, driving an imaginary team of horses. When Crawfie asked Elizabeth if she usually drove in bed, the princess replied, "I mostly go once or twice round the park before I go to sleep....It exercises my horses." Elizabeth was an avid rider while she was growing up, and after she became queen, she used to ride in public on ceremonial occasions. Her last official appearance on a horse was in 1986, when she rode her black mare Burmese (a gift from the Royal Canadian Mounted Police) in her annual birthday parade.

Prince Charles started riding when he was four. He didn't like it at first, but he persevered because his sister, Anne, was good at it. Charles started playing polo (a lethal game played on horseback that is a cross between croquet and hockey) when he was fourteen, after practicing first on a bicycle. He was encouraged in this so-called sport of kings by his father, Prince Philip, who loved to play. (Prince Philip had to give the game up because of arthritis in his wrists, and he turned to four-in-hand carriage driving instead, winning an international driving grand prix when he was sixty-two.) Polo became Charles's passion until a nasty accident in 1990 nearly rearranged the position of his elbow joint. Charles also tried steeplechasing (racing horses over obstacles) for a while, but he gave that up as he had a tendency to fall off his horse.

Princess Anne started riding when she was only two and a half. Both she and her daughter, Zara, are well known for their love of horses. Anne's passion sometimes had humorous results. One night at a formal dinner, she carried on a lengthy, animated conversation about horses with one of the guests. At the end of the meal, she turned to the guest seated on her other side and asked if he would please pass her the sugar. The man solemnly took two cubes of sugar out of the bowl, placed them on the flat of his hand, and offered them to the princess. The pinnacle of Anne's equestrian career was when she was a member of the British team at the 1976 Montreal Olympics.

Princess Anne bought a pony called Trigger for her son, Peter. When Peter outgrew him, Trigger became Prince William's first pony. Harry's first pony, Smokey, was later handed on to his cousins Beatrice and Eugenie. Although both William and Harry were good riders when they were young, nowadays — other than fox hunting — they appear to be more interested in the horsepower to be found under the hood of a car. In 2000, Beatrice and Eugenie made an appearance at a local horse show, showing they are ready to carry on the family tradition. Beatrice, on Del Boy, cleared all the obstacles in her jumping competition, and Eugenie, on a horse named William, came third in the tack and turnout competition.

Many royals of other nationalities have also been accomplished riders. Prince Gustaf Adolf, grandfather of Crown Princess Victoria of Sweden, represented Sweden in the 1936 Berlin Olympics in show-jumping. In 1988, Princess Marthe Louise of Norway competed in two events at the Golden Jubilee Horse of the Year Show at Wembley Arena in London. Princess Haya of Jordan and Prince Albert of Monaco both trained for the 2000 Olympics in Sydney.

Both going to the races and breeding racehorses are pastimes enjoyed by the British royal family — especially Queen Elizabeth and her mother. The Queen Mother specializes in steeplechasers (horses that race over fences), while Queen Elizabeth concentrates on breeding horses that race on the flat. The Queen takes her horse-breeding program very seriously. Once she called in a neurologist (a doctor of the nervous system) to teach Aureole, one of her highly strung thoroughbreds, how to relax. (Another of the Queen's gifted racehorses, Almeria, had dreadful manners in the stable. Almeria once picked up a stable boy by the seat of his pants and dropped him into her manger.) The Ascot races are an important event in the royal social calendar, as are the Badminton Horse Trials, which Princess Anne used to compete in and still likes to attend.

Even royals can't spend all their time outdoors, and royal pets that can be played with inside the house are always popular. Princesses Elizabeth and Margaret had a large white Angora rabbit, which they dressed in a bonnet and shawl and cast as the fairy godmother in their annual Christmas pantomime at Windsor Castle. When he was six, Prince Charles also had a fluffy white rabbit. He called the rabbit Harvey and took very good care of it, cleaning its teeth and cutting its toenails. (His nieces Beatrice and Eugenie were not so successful with their pet rabbits, which had to be taken away when the girls didn't look after them properly.)

The British royal family has never been wild about cats — if you live in grand houses full of old tapestries and antique furniture, there are too many exciting possibilities for sharpening those claws — but they are inordinately fond of their dogs. Even on the day of her coronation in 1837, eighteen-year-old Queen Victoria managed to find time to bathe her King Charles spaniel, Dash. Later, Victoria buried her beloved dogs on the royal estates of Balmoral and Sandringham. The royal family has continued the tradition, and today there are more than 100 dog headstones at Balmoral.

Prince Charles was fond of a yellow Lab called Sandringham Harvey, which was said to have soiled some of the best carpets in England, and of a Jack Russell terrier called Tigger. Tigger had an unusually long curly tail because Charles refused to have it docked in traditional Jack Russell style. Princess Anne once owned a Dumfrieshire hound called Random, which needed a home after it had proved particularly inept at hunting, and a lurcher named Laura. (Lurchers are a special breed of hunting dog, originally bred by poachers to sneak away with game from private country estates.) Beatrice and Eugenie both have Dalmatians. And Prince William owns a Labrador called Widgeon.

Queen Elizabeth has a thing about corgis — little yellow dogs with short legs from Pembrokeshire in Wales. When she was seven, and still a princess, Elizabeth was given a corgi called Dookie (short for "the Duke of York's puppy" because her father was the Duke of York at the time). She had a choice of one with no tail (like most corgis) or another with a stump of a tail. Her mother suggested that Elizabeth should choose the one with a stump. "We must have the one who has something to wag," the Queen Mother said. "Otherwise how are we going to know whether he is pleased or not?"

Today, the Queen usually has a dozen or so corgis in the palace at any one time. Corgis are temperamental dogs, and they are not shy about letting people know if they are feeling out of sorts. Most royal corgis are descended from one called Susan, which accompanied the Queen and Prince Philip on their honeymoon in 1947. Susan is said to have nipped the man whose job it was to wind the hundreds of clocks at Buckingham Palace. Another corgi, called Honey, took the seat out of a guardsman's trousers in 1956. When he was younger, Prince Edward used to think up names for the royal corgis. He sometimes resorted to the obituary notices in the newspaper for inspiration. Among the names chosen over the years (presumably *not* inspired by the obituary notices) were Smoky, Shadow, Myth, Fable, Diamond, and Kelpie.

Not everyone is fond of the Queen's corgis, and sometimes the dogs cause embarrassment to royal guests. Once, at a lunch attended by a woman called Heather, Queen Elizabeth addressed her corgi — also Heather — under the table with a sharp, "Stop it, Heather," giving the other Heather quite a fright. On another occasion, the poet laureate Cecil Day-Lewis put his feet up after a royal luncheon on what he thought was a conveniently placed footstool. It turned out to be a corgi taking a nap.

The Queen Mother shares her daughter's love for this breed of dog. Knowing that, one loyal British subject made the Queen Mother a special tape for her one-hundredth birthday in 2000. It consisted of four corgis — Laila, Zoë, George, and Gina — giving their rendition of "Happy Birthday."

Royal dogs are, of course, pampered. Queen Alexandra's Pekinese was brushed and powdered daily by a palace footman. Queen Elizabeth feeds her corgis herself in her personal apartments. A dust sheet is spread out to protect the royal carpet, and the Queen uses discarded royal dinnerware to serve up the food. Her corgis are never sold, although they may be given away to good homes. When they die, they are buried at Sandringham.

A love of animals was a useful attribute for Prince Edward and his new wife, Sophie Rhys-Jones, when they toured Prince Edward Island in Canada in 2000. Sophie patted the nose of a guinea pig named Max, which had been wrapped up in a blanket and brought by his young owner to downtown Charlottetown to meet with royalty. On the same trip, the royal couple was introduced to a Yorkshire terrier named Sweet Pea, and one woman waiting to greet Edward and Sophie had a large tabby cat draped over her shoulder.

From all of this, you can see that being an animal fan will help you in your quest to become a successful young British royal. A love of sports would also come in handy. First of all, the British royal family is very keen on physical activity, rating it every bit as highly as intellectual pursuits. Second, being royal means you'll have a wonderful opportunity to be coached by the best athletes in the world. (When William and Harry were learning how to play tennis, they had lessons from seven-time Wimbledon champion Steffi Graf, and Charlotte of Monaco received riding instruction from former Olympic equestrian medallist Eric Wauters.) Third, you really need to keep in shape if you are going to get through all those royal engagements without nodding off.

Most young royals take part in team sports at school. Prince Charles used to play rugby, but he was a bit chubby when he was young, and those who got caught underneath him in a scrum would yell, "Get off, fatty." (Not a very nice way to speak to a future king.) He was also captain of the school soccer team for a season, but unfortunately his team didn't win a single game during that time. Later in his school career he did achieve a broken nose in a rugby match — certainly something to write home about.

Team sports are taken very seriously at Eton, the school both William and Harry attended in their teens. In the school handbook, under "What to Do in Case of a Bomb," it reads: "(3) On the playing fields, continue games." I guess you would expect nothing less of a school whose name appears in the famous saying: "The battle of Waterloo was won on the playing fields of Eton." (The saying refers to the competitive spirit instilled in British schoolboys through school sports programs, which made the British such formidable foes on the battlefields of Europe.)

At Eton, both William and Harry played soccer and rugby. Harry was captain of the under-fifteen rugby team. William was a flanker on another team until a broken index finger in 1999 ended his rugby-playing career. He switched to field game, a sport unique to Eton. (It's a cross between rugby and soccer that uses field hockey goals.) William captained his team in the semifinal of a field game tournament. His soccer team also performed well, reaching the semifinals of the school soccer championships. When Harry was fourteen, his father took him on the Eurostar (the train that runs from London to Paris under the English Channel) with 600 other fans to attend a World Cup soccer match in France. Harry and Charles traveled first class in a carriage with six other passengers. England beat Colombia 2–0.

William also played polo at Eton, both on horseback (like his father and grandfather before him) and in the swimming pool. He is an excellent swimmer, as was his mother, Princess Diana, who used to go for a swim in the pool at Buckingham Palace every morning. William was captain of his school's swimming team and the fastest junior swimmer at Eton in ten years. He was the under-sixteen 50-meter (55-yard) freestyle champion in 1997, and the senior 50-meter (55-yard) and 100-meter (110-yard) freestyle champion in 1998. The following year, he came second in the senior diving competition. His warm-up suit was embroidered with the initials W.O.W. (William of Wales).

William's grandfather, Prince Philip, also loves the water, although he prefers it from a boat. Philip had a long and distinguished career in the Royal Navy and likes to sail. Many other European royals are accomplished sailors, too. Ex-King Constantine of Greece won a gold medal sailing in the 1960 Rome Olympics. (Queen Sofia of Spain crewed.) Constantine's daughter Princess Theodora is also a keen sailor. King Juan Carlos of Spain competed for his country in the 1972 Munich games, and his son, Felipe, participated in the 1992 Barcelona Olympics. Prince Harald of Norway participated in sailing regattas in the 1964 Tokyo Olympics. Princess Anne owns her own yacht, *Blue Doublet,* and her children, Peter and Zara, like to help crew. Prince Charles and his family are not so keen on sailing. Charles has a tendency to get seasick, and William and Harry have spent more time cruising the Mediterranean with friends on luxury yachts than they have behind sails.

Winter sports are another area where royals sometimes excel. Prince Michael of Kent was an alternate for the British bobsled team in the 1972 Munich Olympics, and Prince Albert of Monaco represented his country at three different Olympics in bobsled events. Most royals, however, content themselves with winter holidays in luxury resorts in Switzerland and Austria. Prince Harry, in particular, loves to ski. And he likes to go fast! One day when William was eight he burst into tears because he could not keep up with his younger brother on the slopes, and he had to be comforted by his bodyguard.

There is definitely an artistic streak that runs in the British royal family, so if you're not the outdoors, sporty type, perhaps you could be one of the family's more sensitive members. Princess Margaret's governess, Crawfie, believed the princess was a gifted artist, singer, and dancer. Had she not been royal, Crawfie believed Margaret could have considered a career in one of these areas. As it was, her royal duties would take up her time as an adult, and it would not be fitting for her to do anything else. She retains her love of entertaining, though, and often plays the piano at family gatherings.

When Prince Charles was young, he took dance lessons at the palace and apparently was quite an accomplished dancer. To this day he likes to paint, and at school and university he loved to act. Charles played the part of a garbage collector in a comedy skit at university, basing his character on the man who emptied the trash cans near Charles's lodgings at seven every morning, not only creating a dreadful din but singing while he worked. After Charles's performance, the local council changed the time of the college trash collection from seven in the morning to nine. Now that's the kind of influence you can have if you are royal!

Charles's youngest brother, Prince Edward, also enjoyed the arts as a boy. Edward is seventh in line to become king — after Charles and his sons, William and Harry, and Edward's older brother, Andrew, and his daughters, Beatrice and Eugenie. Thanks to the number of relations between Edward and the throne, he has been able to pursue a career in the field he loves. He became the first British prince to be an employee, take home a salary, and be laid off (when his company the Theatre

Division folded). Today Edward runs his own television production company.

An appreciation of the outdoor life will help you in another way as a royal. As most European sovereigns are also the supreme commanders of their country's armed forces, it is expected that young royals — especially boys — will familiarize themselves with military services.

George V, Edward VIII, and George VI were all educated at British Royal Naval colleges. Both David (later Edward VIII) and Bertie (later George VI) saw action during the First World War. Edward made it to the Front in France, over the objections of his father and the government, who pointed out that they didn't want to lose the future king. Edward was unconcerned. "I have four brothers," he reportedly said. He agreed to remain out of harm's way only when Field-Marshal Lord Kitchener told him that the British government's main concern was not that Edward would be killed, but that he might be captured, giving the enemy a strong bargaining position. The future George VI, father of Queen Elizabeth, saw action at the Battle of Jutland in 1916, and his brother, the Duke of Kent, was killed in the line of duty when his plane crashed on a flight to Iceland in 1942. One of the Queen's cousins, the Earl of Harewood, was a prisoner of war during World War II.

During the Second World War, Prince Philip was posted as a midshipman to a battleship in the Mediterranean, and he took part in action off Cape Matapan in March 1941, where the Italian fleet was defeated. He later served on convoys in the North Sea at the rank of first lieutenant. In 1982, Philip's son, Prince Andrew, took part in the Falklands War, when Britain and Argentina were disputing their claims to the Falkland Islands off the coast of Argentina. (The islands are known as the Malvinas to those who claim they belong to Argentina.) Andrew was a second pilot on Sea King helicopters flying anti-submarine and transport duties during the war.

Prince Charles has never seen active service, but he trained with both the Royal Air Force and the Royal Navy. During his training as a jet pilot with the air force, Charles flew as a passenger in a Phantom jet barely 100 meters (400 feet) over Balmoral ("scattering deafened tourists and causing 7 locals to ring up the police in protest," he noted with some satisfaction in his diary). He also became the first British heir to the throne to make a parachute jump. The jump was nearly a disaster, as he got his feet caught in the parachute rigging, but luckily he remained calm and managed to disentangle himself before he hit the ground.

Prince Charles moved on from the Royal Air Force to the Royal Naval College at Dartmouth, where he had a tendency to nod off in his astronavigation classes. He served briefly on a nuclear submarine, which he found very crowded. As he described it, when he turned into his submarine bunk one night, he was surprised by "a grunting and rustling noise somewhere below me and a small officer (I suppose it was!) crawled out sleepily from the bottom bunk like a dormouse emerging from hibernation and disappeared. When I woke up at breakfast time there was somebody else of unknown description hidden by a curtain."

While he was in the navy, Charles qualified as a helicopter pilot, being awarded the Double Diamond trophy for the student who had made the most progress. He was good at flying helicopters, and the newspapers soon began calling him "Action Man." He ended his five-year stint in the navy as captain of the fleet's smallest ship, the wooden-

# Royals and the Military

In most European countries, sovereigns are automatically head of the country's armed forces. In Britain, only the sovereign can declare war or peace (although in these days of constitutional monarchy, the sovereign cannot do this except under the advice of government ministers). When sovereigns made such decisions on their own, they were also expected to lead their troops into battle. The last British sovereign to do this was George II, who defeated the French at the Battle of Dettingen in Germany in 1743. (The last British king to die in battle was Richard III at the Battle of Bosworth in 1485.)

Today, both male and female members of the royal family hold honorary ranks in the armed services. The royals regularly visit the regiments with which they are associated and perform ceremonial inspections of their troops. When Queen Elizabeth was created colonel-in-chief of the Grenadier Guards at the age of sixteen, she took her duties seriously and inspected her troops thoroughly — even taking a good look at the regimental horses' teeth! Elizabeth added an active role to her ceremonial one in 1945 when she joined Britain's Auxiliary Territorial Services, making her the first female member of the British royal family to have been a full-time, active member of the armed forces. All three of her sons, Charles, Andrew, and Edward, served in Britain's armed forces, although only one of them — Prince Andrew — saw action. (He served as a helicopter pilot in the Falklands War in 1982.) Both William and Harry have accompanied their parents to inspect their regiments, and Harry, in particular, is said to be fascinated by the military.

hulled mine hunter HMS Bronington. He acquitted himself well, although he did manage to lose the ship's anchor when it got tangled in an underwater cable. He wrote to his private secretary to explain himself: "For your information — and that of the press office, if necessary — I have just had to slip my starboard anchor, having spent 24 miserable hours trying to free it from an underwater telephone cable....If the press happen to find out, it is something that can occasionally happen and I got rid of the anchor to avoid damage to [the] telephone cable." Luckily for him, the press did not find out at the time. No doubt they would have had a field day with the story.

William and Harry have been fascinated with the military since they were young. After William received a scaled-down uniform from the Parachute Regiment, of which his father was colonel-in-chief, he began saluting anyone he met who was wearing a uniform. He made Harry line up with him at the front door to their apartment in Kensington Palace every morning. Much to Charles's amusement, the two little boys would then snap to attention and salute him as he left for his day's work.

In the summer of 1988, six-year-old William was made a member of the Gordon Highlanders, the regiment that guards Balmoral, for a day. He was dressed in a scaled-down suit of camouflage gear. He was taught how to handle a gun, and he ate lunch with the soldiers in the field kitchen. The best part? "I really love the soldiers' food," he reported back to Harry on his return.

Harry got his turn for a day in the military when he was nine. He flew with his mother to Wisden, Germany, where she was to inspect her regiment — the Light Dragoons. Harry got his face streaked with camouflage paint, wore a scaled-down uniform, rode in a Scimitar tank, and watched a mock battle. William continued his interest in the military and joined Eton's army cadet corps in 1998 when he was sixteen. He received the Sword of Honour, Eton's highest award for a first-year cadet.

Young royals from other countries, both male and female, have also undergone military training. Prince Philippe of Belgium, Duke of Brabant, completed four years' training in the Belgian air force before he began his university studies. Crown Prince Hamzah Al-Hussein, heir to the Jordanian throne, trained as a sniper in the Jordanian army. And Queen Margrethe of Denmark spent four years training with the Danish Royal Women's Air Corps.

The upshot is, no matter what royal family you choose to be born into, you can expect to participate in some kind of outdoor activity. It could be anything from fishing for salmon in a Highland stream to crewing your own boat in a sailing regatta. And don't be surprised if the family sends you off for some military training as well. If you think you won't find this to your taste, take heart — not all young royals like the rigors of military life either. Prince Charles's younger brother, Prince Edward, gave up on his tough training in the British Marines to stick with the arts. Remember, the arts are acceptable pursuits for royals as well. So, brush up on your sailing terminology, sort through your father's fishing tackle box (and pack your paints, just in case), and you're one step closer to being royal.

# SIX

# Entering the Big, Bad World

ONE OF THE HIGHLIGHTS of your growing-up years as a young royal will be your education. Now that governments run countries and many royals just have to show up and look splendid from time to time, academic qualifications are not crucial for the job. A well-rounded education, however, makes for a well-rounded person, and a well-rounded royal will have more to offer his or her country.

The trend among Scandinavian royals is to send their children to local state schools, where they receive the same education as any other citizen of the country. In 1996, Crown Princess Victoria of Sweden graduated at the top of her high school class in Stockholm. Not all royal educations go so well, however. Princess Stephanie of Monaco was expelled from her exclusive French finishing school. (But then Princess Stephanie is not your typical royal. In her adult life she's been a fashion model, a swimsuit designer, and a rock singer.) Just as each young royal is an individual, so royal educations differ widely.

In Britain, the best way to educate the heir to the throne has always been a subject of intense debate. If you are heir, should you be isolated and follow a course of education tailor-made for a king or queen in waiting? Or should you be sent out into the real world so that you can gain a better understanding of the people you are destined to rule? The answer to these questions will affect the course of your education. (The course of your education will also be affected by how smart you are. Since you are born into a royal family and do not have to apply for the position, there is no guarantee that you will be clever or even passably bright.)

Britain's Queen Victoria and Prince Albert were very fond of their children, but they were so determined that their oldest son, the future Edward VII, would become a good king that they devised for him an impossibly rigorous regimen in the palace classroom. Even his tutor thought it was a bit much. "Make him climb trees! Run! Leap! Row!" the tutor implored. However, the queen and Prince Albert took no notice. Edward hardly ever had the opportunity to interact with children other than his brothers and sisters. He used to get so frustrated with his lessons that he would scream and stamp, throw things at walls and through windows, and then collapse in an exhausted heap.

(Victoria and Albert were enlightened in one way, though. In an age when girls were often educated poorly or not at all, they made sure their daughters also got instruction at home.)

Edward's son, George (George V), was second in line to the throne but became the heir when his older brother, Eddy, died of tuberculosis at the age of twenty-eight. George spent most of his formative years in a British naval academy. He came out strong on order, discipline, and tradition but sadly lacking in imagination and general knowledge. As king, George V spent much of his reign trying to fill in the gaps in his knowledge, and he treated his family as though they were a bunch of naval cadets in constant need of discipline. He once said: "My father was frightened of his mother — I was frightened of my father and I am damned well going to see to it that my children are frightened of me."

Even though George knew his own education had been woefully inadequate, he believed strongly in family traditions, and he decided that if an education in the navy had been good enough for him, it would be good enough for his sons as well. So he packed David (Edward VIII) and Bertie (George VI) off to naval college when they were in their early teens and left them there to sink or swim. David emerged a charming playboy. Bertie emerged an earnest young man with a stammer.

(Luckily for Bertie's children, Elizabeth and Margaret, George V made a much better grandfather than he did a parent. Sometimes he would get down on his hands and knees and let his granddaughters unceremoniously lead him along by his beard. They were certainly not in awe of George as his own children had been.)

Because Princess Elizabeth and her sister, Princess Margaret, were born to George V's second son, Bertie, no one expected Elizabeth to one day become queen. If all went according to plan, Bertie's older brother, David, would ascend the throne, marry, and have children of his own. The more children David had, the further down the line of succession Elizabeth and Margaret would be. The education of the princesses, therefore, was not a great concern. (Another reason for the lack of concern was the quaint idea that it was less important to educate girls than it was to educate boys.)

Elizabeth and Margaret's mother wanted them to have "a happy childhood which they [could] always look back on." Their grandmother, Queen Mary, thought that the princesses should "spend as long as possible in the open air, to enjoy to the full the pleasures of the country, to be able to dance and draw and appreciate music, to

# The Abdication of Edward VIII

When George V died in 1936, his oldest son, David, became Edward VIII. The problem was that David didn't really want to be king. He had always hated the stuffiness of the traditions surrounding the royal family, and he disliked ceremonial occasions. The last straw came when he fell in love with a twice-divorced American woman called Wallis Simpson. As the British sovereign is also head of the Church of England, it was not considered proper for a British king to marry a divorced woman (let alone one who had been divorced twice).

Had Edward VIII insisted on marrying Mrs. Simpson, the government would have resigned in protest, causing considerable political unrest, and the British people would have been terribly upset at having a king who set such a bad moral example. (And remember, monarchies only survive these days when the people want them.)

In the end, David decided his love for Mrs. Simpson was greater than his sense of duty or desire to be king, and on December 10, 1936, he abdicated after just 325 days as king so he could marry Mrs. Simpson. His younger brother Bertie was appalled. He had never even seen a state paper in his life, and now he would be expected to deal with them on a daily basis. Despite his misgivings about his training and abilities, Bertie was a determined young man, and with the support and encouragement of his attractive and devoted wife, Queen Elizabeth (the mother of Elizabeth II), he became the well-respected and well-loved King George VI.

acquire good manners and deportment, and to cultivate all the distinctly feminine graces." She also wanted them to learn about their ancestors. Their grandfather, George V, wanted the princesses to have nice handwriting. "For goodness sake, teach Margaret and Lilibet to write in a decent hand," he told their governess. "I like a hand with some character in it."

When Elizabeth was ten, her uncle, King Edward VIII, abdicated
— gave up the throne — in order to marry the woman he loved, and
Elizabeth's father became king. Suddenly Elizabeth was a queen in
the making. The only change to the princess's educational regimen,
however, was the addition of some lessons in constitutional history.
These were given to her by Sir Henry Marten of Eton College. This colorful character kept a pet raven in his study that used to peck him on
the ear. He also kept his pockets full of sugar cubes. During lessons, he
would munch on these absentmindedly in between nibbling on the
corners of his handkerchief.

In 1939, when Princess Elizabeth was thirteen and Princess Margaret was nine, the Second World War broke out, and the princesses left
London for Windsor Castle. Their governess moved with them, and she
set up a Girl Guide troop at the castle so the princesses would have
some other girls their own age to play with. (The Guides got off to a
slow start until the governess persuaded the other girls' mothers that
they should send their daughters to the castle in their uniforms rather
than in their best party clothes.) The princesses lived in relative isolation at Windsor for the next five years. To liven things up a bit, they
organized public Christmas pantomimes and went to parties held in
the castle for local military personnel.

Although Princess Elizabeth had the happy childhood her mother
had wished for her, because of her home schooling and the restrictions
of the war years she had little experience mixing with people outside
the restricted royal circle. Her first real taste of how other people lived
was in 1945, when she persuaded her father to let her join the transport
training center of the Auxiliary Territorial Service, a forerunner of the
Women's Army Corps. In those days, women did not join combat

troops, but they could provide support services back home. The eighteen-year-old princess learned how to strip an engine and drive a military truck. She loved it, and she told her family all about her training in detail. One day soon after she started, Elizabeth's mother reported to a friend, "We had sparking plugs all last night at dinner."

It looked for a while as though Prince Charles too might be taught at home. A Scottish governess, Miss Peebles, was hired when he was five, and Charles began his lessons — all on his own — in the palace. He continued his solitary education until he was finally enrolled in a school outside the palace when he was eight. The Queen, who was reserved in company after her own sheltered upbringing, had decided that future sovereigns should mix with other children and lead more "normal" lives.

When Charles's son, Prince William, trotted off to Mrs. Mynors' Nursery School in Notting Hill Gate, West London, in 1986, he was the first heir to the British throne to go to preschool. In sending William off to school when he was only three, his parents were continuing the royal experiment that Queen Elizabeth and Prince Philip had started — albeit at a later age — with Prince Charles.

On William's first day of school, his mother, Princess Diana, personally drove him there. (The royal detectives followed in another car.) A crowd of photographers was waiting outside the school to snap pictures of the little boy as he grabbed his Postman Pat lunch box, kissed his mother good-bye, and disappeared inside. Diana rushed back from her royal engagement that afternoon — the opening of a dairy — to be waiting for William when he came home.

William was pretty much like any other three-year-old at the school, except that he had no last name. On the school lists, he was identified only as William. (That's one of the curious things about being royal. You don't always have a last name. When Crown Prince Frederik of Denmark went away to Harvard, he needed one so he could be properly registered. As a going-away present, his mother, Queen Margrethe, gave him the last name Henrikson in honor of his father, Prince Henrik.) At Mrs. Mynors's, the lack of a last name was not an impediment. William happily tried to flush a small classmate's lunch box down the toilet, and he and a friend spent one art class painting each other's faces rather than the paper set in front of them.

## What's in a Name?

❧

The odd thing about royals is that even though they have lots of Christian names, they usually go through life without a surname. Prince William is William Arthur Philip Louis. Prince Harry is Henry Charles Albert David. Should they ever need a surname, they would likely use the name Mountbatten-Windsor, which Queen Elizabeth first adopted for her descendants in 1960. Windsor comes from the name of the current branch of the British royal family, the House of Windsor, and Mountbatten is the anglicized version of Prince Philip's mother's maiden name. (If royal families followed the conventions of normal surnames, which they don't, Prince William would likely have his grandfather Prince Philip's name, which — as far as anyone can tell — was something like Schleswig-Holstein-Sonder-burg-Glücksberg-Beck.) The first official use of Mountbatten-Windsor was in 1973 when Princess Anne married, although she signed the marriage register simply "Anne." No surname was included for Prince Charles when he married Diana in 1981 and he signed himself "Charles P." (The "P" stands for Philip, which is Charles's second name.)

William stayed at Mrs. Mynors' for a year before moving on to Wetherby, his first real school. You'd know it was a real English school right away because all the children were wearing uniforms — gray ankle socks, black shorts, white shirt, red tie, and charcoal-gray jacket and matching cap embroidered with the school crest — all bought from Harrods, the big London department store. You'd also notice that all the students were boys. (Although William was being sent to mix with other children, now that he was getting older this mixing did not include little girls.)

Prince Harry followed his brother William to first Mrs. Mynors's and then to Wetherby. (Don't you hate it when you go to the same school as an older brother or sister? "Oh, you must be Mary's little sister. You look just like her!" Or, perhaps more ominously, "So you're Jeremy's younger brother. I hope you don't give us as much trouble as he did!") Harry doesn't seem to have minded much, though. He quite liked having a big brother around who already knew the ropes and could stand up for him if necessary.

William and Harry were sent to school so they could learn to be like other little boys — or like other little rich boys, anyway — but no matter how hard you try to fit in as a young royal, there is always that little something that gives you away. Seeing the royal detective who went wherever William went, one little boy asked why William's dad always came to school with him.

(William and Harry's parents tried to fit in as well, taking part in the parents' races at the school sports day. Diana did very well, coming first in the mothers' fifty-meter (fifty-five-yard) dash. Charles, despite his military training, was a bit of a disappointment, placing last in the fathers' race.)

Although Harry had been thought of as shy at Mrs. Mynors's — he once hid in the playground and refused to join in the other children's games — at Wetherby he gained in self-confidence. At the age of five, he strode confidently onto the stage to sing a solo in the school Christmas concert. His mother was there to hear him.

As a young royal, a love of the stage is certainly an asset, and you can look on your parts in school concerts and plays as being part of your royal training. After all, much of what you do as a royal is a performance for the benefit of the crowd — for a huge crowd, in these days of television. There was great discussion about the wisdom of televising the coronation of Elizabeth II in 1953. There were those who felt it had been bad enough when her parents' wedding ceremony was broadcast over the radio. They worried that "disrespectful people might hear [the royal broadcast] whilst sitting in public houses [bars] with their hats on." Elizabeth, however, felt strongly that people should have the opportunity to experience the ceremonies, even if they could not be there in person. Since 1953, many royal occasions have been televised to audiences around the world, including weddings and birthday celebrations.

The ceremony to publicly present Prince Charles as the Prince of Wales at Caernarvon Castle in 1969 was an event specifically designed for television. The clear canopy that covered the royal platform was made of an acrylic material called Perspex. It weighed over a tonne (ton) and at the time was the largest Perspex object ever made. During the ceremony, Charles realized to his horror that he was sitting on the pages of his speech, and he had to wiggle them out from under his robes as unobtrusively as possible.

One of the most lavish royal shows in London recently was the parade to celebrate Queen Elizabeth the Queen Mother's 100th birthday. For an hour and a half, a procession of more than 6,000 people entertained the royal family. Stunt planes colored the sky red, white, and blue. Army bands and the Royal Philharmonic Orchestra provided the music. A million rose petals were dropped from the scaffolding behind the royal party to end the day.

One of the highlights of the parade was six members of the Worshipful Company of Grocers — an association of merchants of which the Queen Mother is an honorary member — who rode by on camels. (Camel trains were used to transport spices in medieval times, and the company traces its origins back to the Guild of Pepperers, who traded spices in those days.) Before the parade, it was feared that the camels might frighten the horses in the procession or that one of the camels might bolt. The horses stayed calm and no camel ran away, but one of them did keep dropping to its knees as though in an inelegant curtsy, holding up the parade and worrying its rider.

In 1987, in their continuing effort to get the young royals to mix more with other children, Charles and Diana sent five-year-old William and three-year-old Harry to play with a group of children in a working-class neighborhood in London. It was supposed to be a secret visit. But when a girl asked William his name, and his detective told her William was called Roger, William immediately blew his cover by correcting the man. As luck would have it, William did have an opportunity to perform a royal gesture that day. "A gerbil ran down my back and William grabbed it off. I was very grateful," reported one Anastasia Harrison, aged eleven.

It has always been a problem figuring out how to help young royals get to know children from different backgrounds. Hansell, who was the tutor to George V's sons, David and Bertie, decided sports might be the way to go, and he arranged a soccer game for the princes with some local boys. There was a problem, though: the local boys were so in awe of the princes that they didn't dare go anywhere near them, in case they kicked David and Bertie by mistake.

A policeman at Sandringham found himself in a similar dilemma one winter when young Prince Charles started throwing snowballs at him. The policeman decided it was most probably not a good idea to hit the future king with a cold wet one. But when Charles's father, Prince Philip, witnessed this interaction, he was exasperated. "Don't just stand there," he shouted to the policeman. "Throw some back."

When Charles was told at age seven that he would be going to Hill House school with other schoolboys, he asked, "Mummy, what *are* schoolboys?" As he was soon to find out, whatever they were, they were not quick to welcome him. A fellow student at one of Charles's later schools said, "How can you treat a boy as just an ordinary chap when his mother's portrait is on the coins you spend in the school shop, on the stamps you put on your letters home, and when a detective follows him wherever he goes? Most boys tend to fight shy of friendship with Charles. The result is that he is very lonely." (Charles's life was made marginally easier at his next school, Cheam, when the Association of Retail Confectioners of America got wind of a story that Charles's allowance from his parents was so stingy that he couldn't afford to buy candy. They sent him a huge care package of American confectionery, which made him very popular.)

In an effort to get her son Prince Andrew to mix with boys his age, Queen Elizabeth signed him up with the Cub Scouts. It was decided, however, that the Scouts should come to Andrew, rather than

Andrew going to the Scouts. This meant that all the so-called adventure activities took place in Andrew's backyard, which nobody found very stimulating.

By the time they were eight — the age at which their father first left the palace for his schooling — both William and Harry were already onto their third school, Ludgrove. Its job is to prepare little boys for one of the most prestigious schools in Britain, Eton.

Ludgrove is a boarding school. When the boys arrive at the beginning of term, they stay there — even on most weekends — until the school term is over. You might think that this is some special treatment reserved for British royals, but there you would be wrong. Boarding schools are popular in Britain, where it is not considered strange to send eight-year-old children away from home for extended periods of time.

Neither William nor Harry got special treatment at Ludgrove. The only giveaway to mark them as princes was the ever-present bodyguards (now a rotating team of eighteen). Both William and Harry slept in dormitories with five other boys, used a communal washroom, and were allowed home just once a month. And — an important landmark for boys in British schools — long pants finally became a part of their school uniform, signaling that they had left their elementary school days behind them.

(One of the curious things about going to school when you are a royal is that a lot of the history lessons are about your family. It's a bit like taking all the family skeletons out of the closets. You have to hope that the rest of the class doesn't start comparing you to your ancestors, wondering if you will chop off your wives' heads like Henry VIII, be run out of the country like James II, or go mad like George III.)

William and Harry may not have received any special treatment at school, but their home lives were pretty special. Prince William's eighth birthday party was held at the insect house in London Zoo. His birthday cake, in keeping with the zoo theme, was in the shape of an elephant.

## Royal Birthday Bashes

Royal birthdays are often an opportunity for extravagance. A fancy dress party was held to celebrate the first birthday of Prince William's cousin Princess Beatrice. The party was held on the lawns of Castlewood House, and more than 100 guests were invited. The little guests were asked to dress up as ragamuffins and their nannies dressed up as dragons. There were races and prizes, a bouncy castle to jump on, and lots of mustard and ketchup for the birthday hamburgers. When Beatrice turned nine she got to take fifteen friends to Disneyland Paris (now Euro Disney). The cost? A mere $15,000. When Prince Albert of Bavaria was nine, his mother took him to the opening concert of Michael Jackson's world tour in Munich as a birthday treat. After the concert, Albert rode with the star on his motorcycle, and two days later, Michael Jackson and the young prince went to Euro Disney. And when you are a royal teenager, things can get even more exciting. As a treat for Prince Harry's thirteenth birthday, his father, Prince Charles, invited the Spice Girls to tea at his country estate. The band flew in by helicopter and stayed for a couple of hours. (Harry had previously attended a Spice Girls concert in South Africa and had met the band backstage after the London premiere of their movie *Spice World*.)

William and Harry also got the opportunity to travel during their school holidays. In 1991, Charles and Diana paid an official visit to Canada, and William and Harry flew out to meet them. Diana's greeting for the two boys was very different from the one Queen Elizabeth had given Prince Charles in Tobruk all those years ago: Diana dropped to her knees with outstretched arms as soon as she saw her sons. The reunion took place aboard the royal yacht, *Britannia,* which was moored in Lake Ontario near Toronto.

William (nine) and Harry (seven) had a number of adventures on this trip. They toured HMCS *Ottawa,* which was escorting *Britannia,* and playfully turned its fifty-caliber, twin-barreled guns onto a nearby police launch. The police officers raised their hands in mock surrender. Then they got to take the controls of the Canadian Forces Corvair that flew them from Toronto to Sudbury. They also got to steer the boat that took them through the spray at Niagara Falls, the *Maid of the Mist.* Harry wanted to take the boat right under the falls until the captain explained to him that if they did, they would never get out again! The boys were flown back to Toronto by helicopter, and they got to try on the helmets belonging to the air crew.

In between parties and trips, Princess Diana did what she could to treat her boys as normal children. She made them line up in Marks & Spencers, a popular British store, to pay for their purchases. She took them to movies at theaters in London's Leicester Square, for messy meals of spareribs at the Chicago Rib Shack, and for the occasional burger at McDonald's. Like other children, William and Harry stood in line for the rides at Thorpe Park, an amusement park in Kent, and for the chance to see Santa at Christmas. When the Santa Claus at the London department store Selfridges asked Prince Harry what he wanted as a present, the young prince replied, "A piece of Christmas cake." William, aged four, was rather suspicious. He asked Santa: "What are you doing here? We saw you at Harrods last Friday."

But even though Diana made an effort to show her boys how other children lived, these excursions were occasional diversions from the princes' privileged lives. She had no trouble getting William and Harry the best seats in the house for a London production of *Joseph and the Amazing Technicolor Dreamcoat,* even though the popular West End show was supposedly sold out. On the day of the men's singles tennis finals at the prestigious All-England Tennis Club at Wimbledon, Prince William had a front-row seat with his mother in the royal box. And William and Harry got the royal treatment when they visited Disney World in Orlando, Florida, on their summer holidays in 1993. (William was eleven and Harry was eight.) Their convoy of unmarked cars was escorted from the airport by Orange County deputy sheriffs. Once in the theme park, the royal party used hidden tunnels to get around, and the rides were closed to other visitors while they were enjoying them. Their $1,450-a-night presidential suite at the Grand Floridian hotel was accessible only by private elevator, which kept them safe from all the tourists and reporters hoping to get a glimpse of the royals.

Exciting trips, great birthday parties, no line-ups, and luxury hotels certainly seem like good reasons to want to be born royal. But while some of these perks come about because of your privileged position, others come from the need to keep you safe. As a royal, you must be constantly on your guard, which is why personal detectives follow you everywhere you go.

Threats to royal security are not a modern phenomenon. When Victoria was queen, a seventeen-year-old boy snuck into Buckingham Palace by climbing over a wall and creeping in through an open window. He said he meant no harm. He just wanted to know what life in the palace was like — and he thought what he learned might make a good book. (Now there was a boy ahead of his time!)

Victoria's young man was only one of a number of people who have found their way into the palace over the years. During the First World War, a distressed deserter turned up in Queen Elizabeth the Queen Mother's bedroom. He promptly threw himself at the queen's feet and began pouring out his troubles to her. She soothingly encouraged him to "tell her all about it" while she edged her way toward the emergency bell.

Elizabeth's daughter, Queen Elizabeth II, experienced a similar incident one night in 1982, when an unemployed man climbed into her bedroom window at Buckingham Palace and sat on the end of her bed. At first, the Queen could not summon help because her footman was out exercising a dozen corgis, the security guard in the corridor had gone off duty at six, the housemaid was busy cleaning another room, and no one was taking any notice of the emergency buzzer, thinking it had gone off by mistake. When the intruder asked for a cigarette, the Queen calmly said that she would send for some. This time she did manage to alert palace employees.

Princess Anne was the victim of a far more serious incident in 1974, when a man tried to kidnap her at gunpoint as she was riding in a car. The twenty-four-year-old Anne grabbed the car door handle, held the door shut, and refused to get out. The man fired six shots, injuring the chauffeur, Anne's bodyguard, a policeman, and a passerby who had stopped to help. Anne's father, Prince Philip, later said proudly, "If the man had succeeded in abducting Anne, she'd have given him the hell of a time."

Royal security is a full-time job. Some royal bodyguards wear uniforms. (The one who sits outside the Queen's door at night wears a slightly adapted uniform: he dons slippers instead of boots so as not to disturb the royal slumbers.) Other bodyguards blend in with the crowd. When William and Harry took that trip to Disney World in 1993, the U.S. Secret Service agents assigned to protect them were dressed up as cartoon characters.

When royals travel, a supply of the correct blood type accompanies them in case of emergencies. And it is customary for members of the immediate royal family to fly on separate planes. That way, if one of the planes has an accident, at least some of the family is left to carry on.

Royal homes are wired with security alarms, and security officers are given detailed layouts of each room, showing even the position of the furniture. This means that royals cannot rearrange their rooms without first alerting their security forces. In case of emergency, rescue squads don't want to be banging their shins against unexpected tables or blundering into cabinets full of priceless china. All royals also undergo some basic training in self-defense and learn how to react during a hostage-taking or assassination attempt.

As a young royal, you'll find that security concerns can seriously cramp your style. Prince Albert of Bavaria used to be driven to school in a bulletproof Mercedes by a different route every day. He was not allowed to get out of the car until the parking lot had been thoroughly checked by guards. When Prince William was eight, he was handed an electronic homing device to wear — just like the one used to track people under house arrest. This measure was considered necessary after William took off on his pony on the Balmoral estate one day and nobody could find him. One of the drawbacks to wearing this device, he soon discovered, was that it gave his personal detective an unfair advantage when they played hide-and-seek.

# SEVEN

# Mad about Royals

AS A YOUNG ROYAL, you will not only need to be protected from people who want to kidnap you or (as in the case of the Queen Mother and the Queen) drop by your place for a little chat, you will also need to be protected from the media.

The relationship between royals and the media is a tricky balancing act. A monarchy lasts only as long as people want one for their country. Once citizens lose interest in their kings and queens, disagree with their monarchs' behavior, or embrace a political system that has no room for a monarchy, they often ask the royal family to leave. There are many royal families scattered around the world who would love to be invited back to rule. The families of the ex-sovereigns of Brazil, Greece, Romania, and Yugoslavia are all waiting to see if one day their countries will decide they'd like a monarchy again. Some, like the Italian royal family, would be content with just being allowed to return home as ordinary citizens. (Since they voted out their monarchy in 1946, Italians have banned members of their former royal family from setting foot on Italian soil.)

One way to maintain people's interest in the monarchy is to have the royal family's activities reported in newspapers and on television, so that citizens can see how the royals are spending their time. As Britain's Prince Charles once said: "It's when people stop reading and talking about us that we will have to start worrying." The problem, though, is that the media often become intrusive, too insistent on poking into every corner of royal lives.

Unwanted media attention can be extremely unpleasant. As a royal, you need to be prepared for the fact that everything you do or say might appear next day on the front page of the newspaper. Journalists often feel they can give you advice on how you ought to be living your royal life — telling you how you should behave and even criticizing your taste in clothes. And sometimes hounding by the media becomes downright dangerous. There are those who say that the photographers who were chasing after Princess Diana in Paris contributed to her fatal car crash in 1997.

Too much media attention can also dilute the appeal of the royal family. If the media strip away royal mystery and reveal too many shortcomings, the people of the country in question may decide their monarchy is not special enough to be worth keeping. The trick, then, is to find the right balance. As a royal, you need enough media coverage to maintain people's interest, but not so much that people get intimately acquainted with all your faults.

The media have problems of their own when it comes to reporting on the royals. The first problem has to do with timing. To stay in business, news directors at radio and television stations and editors at newspapers must find ways to attract audiences — and preferably larger audiences than their competitors can command. To do this, they need bigger and better stories, and they need to be the first ones to make them public. This means there is tremendous pressure to broadcast or publish stories even if those responsible for airing them can't be 100 percent certain that the stories are true.

The second problem has to do with the depth of coverage. The media argue that because the royal family survives through the will of the people, its members are, to some extent, public property, and people have a right to know the details of their lives. There are always stories, however, that are on the borderline between responsible reporting and unwarranted intrusion. What to publish and what not to publish is a judgment call, and the line that divides the two is never crystal clear.

Just how far reporters should go to get their stories is equally ill defined. After Diana's death in 1997, British journalists generally agreed not to pursue William and Harry in the way they had pursued the boys' mother. The British Press Complaints Commission declared that no photos of the princes could appear in the media without Prince Charles's consent — unless there was "exceptional public interest." But it has never been determined who has the authority to decide what is of exceptional interest to the public, and this issue is still unresolved.

There are constant meetings between the media and officials at Buckingham Palace as both sides try to agree on the rules of the game. Palace officials attempt to negotiate media-free time for the royals in return for officially sanctioned photo opportunities and interviews. But even when the media agree, there is always someone who will push the limits to get an exclusive photograph or story. The whole thing turns into an elaborate game of hide-and-seek, in which each side tries to outwit the other.

Journalists stake out houses around the clock if they suspect a royal might come out. They use binoculars to read lips. They try to get the servants to talk. For their part, royals conceal their travel plans,

## Royal Fashion

❧

The media is quick to comment on what royals are wearing. During Princess Diana's lifetime, reporters always commented on her outfits and which designers were supplying her clothes. As a royal, a constant supply of new clothes for formal occasions is a must, and you will have to get used to people crawling about on their hands and knees in front of you with pins in their mouths as they fix a ruffle or adjust a hemline.

Because royals are so heavily photographed, ardent royal watchers are quick to notice if royals recycle clothes. (Princess Anne is well known for her frugal approach to her wardrobe and can often be spotted in a dress that has been worn on more than one royal occasion.) Although the media can be cruel about what royals are wearing — for instance, photographing Diana with the sun shining through her skirt to reveal her legs or

commenting on Sarah Ferguson's latest unbecoming outfit — they can also be surprisingly generous in their comments. When Prince Charles was four, he was named one of the world's ten best-dressed men by *Tailor and Cutter* magazine, which gave him top marks for his taste in "baby bows, farm stalkers, and double-breasted cardigans." And on a trip to Italy in 2000, the press positively drooled over Queen Elizabeth's

travel in different cars, and use back entrances to give photographers the slip. When Sweden's King Carl XVI Gustav was courting his wife-to-be, Silvia Sommerlath, in 1975, he hired a royal look-alike to distract journalists, and Ms. Sommerlath took to dressing up in a wig and dark glasses to throw them off track. When Queen Beatrix of the Netherlands went to the hospital to give birth to her first child in 1967, she used an armored car to make it through the ranks of journalists.

Unfortunately, exclusive photographs sell for huge amounts of money, so people will go to considerable lengths to photograph royals sophisticated dress sense and devoted much discussion to her discriminating taste in purses. (Despite their enthusiasm, I bet you wouldn't be seen dead with one of those stodgy little items over your arm. And, in case you were wondering, that's where the queen keeps her lipstick, but not much else.)

One of the reasons the press is so interested in what royals wear is that a wider range of outfits makes for more interesting photographs, the currency in which press photographers trade. The photographers who follow Prince Charles and his sons on their skiing holidays every year often complain because Charles always wears a gray one-piece ski suit. Charles knows the photographers don't like this and one year brought it to their attention that he was wearing a new suit. It was still a uniform grayish number, though, and photographers had to resign themselves to the fact that Charles has not fulfilled his early fashion potential. Both William and Harry show promise in this area. They are often smartly turned out in expensive shirts and well-tailored jackets and pants, but they also have moments when they show their individual fashion flair: Harry sports bandannas as part of his skiing attire, and William has been photographed wearing distinctive, colorful waistcoats.

when they least expect it. In 1982, a photographer traveled to the Bahamas to get a shot of Diana while she was pregnant with William. After crawling through the jungle with heavy camera equipment for an hour and a half and then sitting around waiting for another three and a half hours, he was rewarded with a shot of Diana wearing a bikini and rubbing suntan oil on Charles's back. The photographer was later quoted as saying, "I've never done anything as intrusive in my life, but it was a journalistic high. I've never had such a buzz."

Other journalists crawl around in the bushes closer to home.

When Charles was at his second school, Cheam, the headmaster's daughter noticed some strange lights in shrubbery on the school grounds one evening. They turned out to be the lights on the camera of a French journalist who was using infrared technology to take pictures of Charles's school after dark. Charles's son William was also the victim of a photographer crawling around in the bushes near his first school. The photographer snapped some fuzzy shots of William taking a surreptitious pee, but only one newspaper editor decided the shots were sufficiently newsworthy to warrant publication. On another occasion, a photographer caught a young Prince William trying to pinch a female teacher's bottom.

The struggle between the royals' right to privacy and the public's right to know has been going on at least since the time of Queen Victoria. In 1848, Victoria and her husband, Prince Albert, sued a man who had published reproductions of etchings depicting the royal family's private life. Victoria and Albert won, establishing the legal precedent that an artistic work cannot be reproduced without the permission of the artist.

William and Harry, along with their cousins Beatrice and Eugenie, have been exposed to the media practically from the day they were born. (And William from even *before* the day he was born, if you count the shots of a pregnant Diana in her bikini.) In 1988, when Sarah, Duchess of York, appeared on the steps of Portland Hospital with baby Beatrice in her arms, an estimated 600 photographs were taken within the first minute. When Sarah arrived home from the hospital with her second daughter, Eugenie, in 1990, she found the official photographer already waiting for her with his lights up and backdrops in place.

Buckingham Palace, recognizing William's importance to the

nation as the future king, agreed to official photo shoots marking milestones in his life: his christening, for instance, and his birthdays. On the official shoot for William's second birthday, Charles drew his son's attention to the microphones everywhere. "Those are the big sausage things which record everything you say — start learning," he said.

If you are a young royal, your parents will do their best to educate you about the media. Princess Anne was shocked to find that photographers had offered her son Peter 10p (about 15 cents) to pose for them at the Badminton Horse Trials one year. She immediately took the money away and gave him a lesson in royal relations with the media. Princess Diana sometimes used to shout at those she felt were getting too close to her sons. She once rolled down the window of her car and yelled at photographers who were trying to get a photo of William leaving Kensington Palace: "Leave him alone! Alone, do you hear! How would you like your children to be treated like that?"

Family is extremely important if you are a young royal, because the attention you attract clearly sets you apart from other people. Your family — even if you are not getting on with the people in it very well — is a support system. From an early age, if you have royal brothers and sisters, you will be encouraged to confide in them rather than in your friends. This is partly because no one else can really appreciate what you are going through and partly because you never know when your friends might decide to sell their stories to the press. On top of it all, it is sometimes difficult to tell exactly who your friends are. Do the people who rush to greet you like you as a person, or do they just want to get close to you because you are royal? Sometimes the problem is not overpopularity: it is being shunned by those around you. Prince Charles was often lonely at school as boys were reluctant to approach

# Royal Family Dynamics

❧

In the days of the absolute monarchy, there was as much danger to a young royal from within the family as there was from without, since people were constantly figuring out who was next in line for the throne and seeing what they could do to improve their chances of becoming king or queen. Take the famous British king Henry VIII, for example — he went through six wives in his quest for a male heir. (He divorced his first and fourth wives; he had the second and fifth executed; his third wife died; and the sixth one had the good fortune to outlive him.) King Richard III, whose reign lasted only from 1483 to 1485, was accused of murdering his young nephews in his own bid for power. Relationships between siblings were often tense as well. Mary I imprisoned her sister, later Elizabeth I, for long periods during her reign, because she was afraid the popular Elizabeth would lead an uprising against her.

Since the time of Queen Victoria, when sovereigns were relinquishing their political powers and easing into more purely ceremonial positions, the British royals have stressed the importance of a close, supportive family life. Victoria and Albert had nine children, and they loved nothing better than to escape to Osborne, their home on the Isle of Wight, to spend time with their children. George VI, the present queen's father, and his wife went out of their way to present a model royal family to the nation. This sense of family closeness has begun to fray at the edges as the first marriages of three of the Queen's four children have ended in divorce (only Edward, her youngest, has escaped this fate). But, since the death of Princess Diana in 1997, Prince Charles has proved himself to be a supportive and loving father, and it is clear from photographs taken in the late 1990s that he and his sons have forged a strong bond.

him. He would ask himself: "What's wrong? Do I smell? Have I changed my socks?"

It's difficult to gauge what other people think of you even in uncomplicated situations. Think of the agonies you'd go through as a young royal trying to figure out if that popular boy at the back of the class is avoiding you because he doesn't like you or because he's a decent sort and just doesn't want to intrude. Maybe you should make the first move. But then it might look as though you were throwing your royal weight around, and if he's a nice guy he'll be turned off right away. This kind of second-guessing would be guaranteed to keep you awake nights!

You will be relieved to know that royal sibling relationships are pretty much like sibling relationships in any other family. Sometimes you get along. Sometimes you don't. Princess Elizabeth used to complain that her younger sister always wanted what Elizabeth wanted, and the two girls would sometimes get into awful fights. Elizabeth would punch her younger sister and Margaret would bite back. Charles and Anne also used to hit each other. Their father once bought boxing gloves, thinking that he would teach Charles how to box. When he saw Charles and Anne using them on each other, he decided he'd better take them away before serious damage was done.

Royal children usually accept that — barring unusual circumstances — only one of them will get to reign. And if you are born into a royal family where boys take precedence, it is not always the oldest who inherits the throne. The heir to the throne in Spain, Infante Felipe, Prince of the Asturias, has two older sisters, the Infantas Elena and Christina. The girls seem to have borne their younger brother no ill will when the three of them were growing up, despite his position of precedence, and they are reported to have spoiled him dreadfully.

William and Harry have always been close. Harry looks up to William, and William looks after Harry. Once, on a day out with their father, Prince Charles, at Windsor Safari Park when William was six, William shouted up to four-year-old Harry — who was about to tackle a giant slide — "Harry, Harry, take your coat off. You will go much quicker." If there are tense moments between them, it is usually when Harry, who is more adventurous than his older brother, takes off and leaves William behind. (None of us likes it when we are shown up by a younger member of the family!)

It is fortunate that William and Harry are so close, because young royals know they have to be careful what they say outside the family. You can't always reveal your innermost thoughts to your friends. When William wrote to a school friend after he had an accident at school, he warned his friend to lock the letters away so that they wouldn't fall into "enemy hands."

Intense media attention can make it very difficult for you to do many things that less-well-known people find perfectly normal. Take, for instance, the simple issue of going to school. When eight-year-old Prince Charles tried to pursue his education outside Buckingham Palace, photographers and journalists camped outside the school he was attending, Hill House, and refused to leave. They gave up only after palace officials personally telephoned all the editors and told them that if the photographers and journalists did not go away, the Queen would have to abandon her ideas for educating Charles at a regular school. Not only was it not fair to Charles to have all those photographers and journalists hanging around, it wasn't fair to the other students, either.

Charles's trials with the media continued on and off throughout his school days. When he was thirteen, he was sent to Gordonstoun, a school in the Scottish Highlands that prided itself on turning boys into men. His father had attended Gordonstoun, but another reason Charles went there was that the school was far from the prying eyes of the London media. Despite the school's isolation, there were a couple of incidents there that gave Charles a lifelong suspicion of journalists.

On one occasion, one of his school notebooks was stolen and sold to a newspaper in Germany. The British press did not print any of it, but an essay he had written did appear in translation in a German magazine, *Der Stern*. (It's bad enough having your teachers read and mark your essays. Imagine what it would be like to have them published in newspapers so that everybody could read them!) An American magazine, *Time,* picked up a related story that Charles might have sold the essay (and on another occasion his autograph) because he was short of ready cash.

The incident that most upset Charles became known as the cherry brandy incident. The fourteen-year-old Prince of Wales was on a week's cruise in the Outer Hebrides as part of a school exercise in seamanship. During a break from sailing, Charles was sitting in a hotel in Stornoway, on the Isle of Lewis, when he saw a crowd peering in the windows at him. He decided to seek refuge in the relative privacy of the hotel bar. Once there, the flustered Charles thought he ought to order a drink. (That's what you do in a bar, isn't it?) Charles ordered a cherry brandy because he had had some to warm up while on a shooting party. As he was having his drink, a reporter came in. Newspapers around the world soon printed the story that the underage heir to the British throne had consumed an alcoholic beverage in a public bar. Charles was disciplined at school, and his detective was reassigned. Thoroughly humiliated by the international attention, he realized he would always have to be on his guard against reporters in the future.

One of the positive effects of Charles's experiences at school is that today there is an agreement with the press that all schoolchildren in Britain must be allowed their privacy, whether they are royal or not. When William and Harry went to Eton, their fellow students were told they would be expelled if they spoke with reporters about the princes, and the press honored their agreement with the palace to leave the princes alone. (At the age of eighteen, however, the princes would once again be fair game.)

Even though William and Harry had some protection from the media while away at school, the press certainly did not give them an easy time of it during their growing-up years. One reason for this was the incredible popularity of their beautiful and fashionable mother, Princess Diana. Later, the deterioration of Charles and Diana's marriage became a royal soap opera that was reported on almost daily in the press.

Even before the press knew about the problems Charles and Diana were having, they had been quick to criticize Charles's parenting skills. One reporter wrote that Charles was a distant father who treated his sons "like well-fed pets." An incident in which a schoolmate accidentally bashed William on the head with a golf putter fueled this feeling about Prince Charles. After the accident, William was taken to hospital, where doctors decided to operate. They wanted to push out the slight indentation the golf putter had left in William's skull and check for bone splinters. After satisfying himself that it was a relatively minor operation, Charles left William's mother, Diana, in charge and kept an appointment to attend the opera with government ministers. The next morning, Charles telephoned to see how William was doing, then attended an environmental conference in the north of England before returning to London to visit his son. The British press had a field day. "What Kind of a Dad Are You?" screamed the headlines in the *Sun*. The *Daily Express* wrote: "What sort of a father of an eight-year-old boy, nearly brained by a golf club, leaves the hospital before knowing the outcome for a night at the opera?"

(Imagine for a moment what it would be like if the media were always there ready to pass judgment on your parents' parenting skills — or, worse yet, on your performance as your family's hope for the future. What kind of headlines might that give rise to? "Allowance Denied Because of Messy Bedroom!"? "Young Royal Refuses to Walk the Dog"?)

Media reports of Charles's distance from his sons continued. On one holiday break from school, William rushed into Charles's office in Kensington Palace and burst into tears when he found that his father was not there. Diana telephoned Charles at Balmoral to let him know what had happened, and Charles welcomed his son home with a hand-written fax. Charles also missed many school events, including Harry's solo at the school Christmas concert. And when the family spent week-ends at their estate in the country, Charles retreated to his walled garden, which was off-limits to little boys.

The more his marriage deteriorated, the more distant Charles became. As the older son, William found himself providing emotional support to his often-distraught mother, handing her tissues under the bathroom door when she locked herself in for a good cry. He found the whole situation so stressful that he too would lock himself in the bath-room for hours, and his grades at school took a nose-dive. When William said he wanted to become a policeman so he could protect his mother, Harry pointed out that he couldn't, because he had to be king. When it became clear that Charles and Diana's marriage was not salvageable, Diana traveled to Ludgrove boarding school to break the news to the boys. They were summoned to the headmaster's office to hear what their mother had to say. William cried and Harry was stoically silent.

Prince Philip once said that the problem with royal children is not educating them, it is bringing them up as people. The one thing you may have noticed in all this discussion about being royal is that, although the lifestyle comes with some major perks, you are still a person who reacts to positive and negative events in your life in the same way that other people do. Your personal detectives may shield you from physical harm, but there is nothing they can do to protect you from emotional ups and downs. Not only did William and Harry have to go through the painful process of their parents' separation and divorce, but the media attention ensured that everybody else in the world could take a front-row seat in the drama.

Many children have parents whose marriages break down. If you've been in this situation yourself — or have watched any of your friends go through it — you know how hard it can be to witness your parents hurting each other. Imagine, then, the horror of seeing reports of their arguments printed in the papers or hearing their behavior discussed on the radio. Even worse for William and Harry, their parents aired their opposing sides of the story on television. Luckily for the two young princes, no one in the press was allowed to ask them what they thought about it all. (Although photographers are always lying in wait for whatever royals they can get their telescopic lenses on, journalists do not approach young royals for interviews or comments. That, at least, is one area in which royals have control. The Queen Mother has only ever given one interview — and that was right after she married into the royal family. She didn't do it again, because her new father-in-law, King George V, expressed his displeasure. Although Prince Charles speaks to journalists from time to time to give his views on an issue, the Queen never, ever gives interviews — not even to set the record straight.)

Newspapers were scarce at Ludgrove, William and Harry's school, and television broadcasts were monitored, but William did have a radio. It was an extremely stressful situation to be in — away from home and torn between warring parents whose embarrassingly bad behavior was widely reported. It would be enough to make anyone want to hide away forever. But as royal children, William and Harry still had to be seen in public. That's one of the key lessons of being brought up royal. No matter what is going on in your private life, you have to put on a brave face for the media — especially in Britain, the land of the "stiff upper lip." The press are constantly watching for signs of weakness, stories they can tell, and juicy gossip they can spread.

After Charles and Diana separated, the boys divided their time between their parents. It was almost as though they were different children depending on which parent they were with. Diana would dress the boys casually in designer clothes and take them to movies, go-kart tracks, and amusement parks. Her idea of the ideal holiday was somewhere sunny and warm. Charles would take his sons shooting and fishing or outfit them in dress pants, jackets, and ties for weekends at his country estate. His idea of the ideal holiday was a relaxing break tramping across the misty moors of Balmoral. In public, Diana was demonstrative with her sons, often hugging them in front of the cameras. Charles, for his part, said he was not a monkey and wouldn't "perform" for the press.

## The Horrors of the Press

The media pretty much left Prince William and Prince Harry alone when they were at school or on vacation with their family on the British royal estates. As soon as the princes left these havens of security, however, the media was there to get them. One skiing holiday with their mother at the Austrian resort of Lech in 1993 was particularly horrendous. Photographers were crawling all over the mountain. They were in the restaurant where the royal family had lunch, and about thirty of them were waiting outside the supermarket where Diana was shopping. When the media horde closed in on her as she tried to cross the street to get back to the hotel, a Scotland Yard protection officer decided it was time to make a move. He lunged out at one photographer, and both of them ended up on the ground while William and Harry looked on in dismay. Another time, the shock of having French cameramen closing in around the royal car, which had come to a stop on the roadside, made Harry nauseated. It took him a day to recover from the incident.

The media think nothing of making something up if they are facing a tough deadline and need a good lead. These stories are especially hot when journalists suspect romantic liaisons. George V joked to his fiancée, May (later Queen Mary), in the late nineteenth century that he would have to call their wedding off as, according to the media, he was already a married man with three children. Before Charles became involved with Diana, it was erroneously reported that he was having a romance with the Duke of Wellington's daughter. Following stories about the "romance" in the media, 10,000 people turned up to watch the pair going to church at Sandringham. Charles joked that perhaps he should get married out of a feeling of obligation to the public. "Such was the obvious conviction that what they had read was true that I almost felt I had better espouse myself at once so as not to disappoint so many people." (Before Queen Beatrix of the Netherlands married her husband when she was twenty-seven, she was linked by the media with no fewer than 215 suitors.)

Speculating about likely mates for Prince William, one news story reported that he and one Isabella Anstruther-Gough-Calthorpe "enjoyed a close bond." The two young people had never actually met. But never letting reality stand in the way of a good story, a betting firm had Ms. Anstruther-Gough-Calthorpe as the 5–1 favorite to be the future queen of Britain.

In the face of such intense pressure, humor is often the only response that keeps royals sane. Once during Charles's navy days, the press was looking for him on HMS *San Diego,* which was docked in California at the time. A ship's officer approached by the journalists told them: "I'm certainly not going to disturb the prince. He gets angry at the slightest disturbance; he's big-headed, pompous and stupid… believes he's king already and treats us like valets." The officer, as it turned out later, had been none other than the prince himself!

On another foreign visit, this time in Canada, Charles was wearing an insulated wetsuit in order to make a dive in Arctic waters without freezing to death. To the amazement of the press corps following him, he proceeded to demonstrate how he could make himself look like an animated balloon by filling the wetsuit with air.

By the age of seventeen, Prince William was also beginning to see the funny side of security and the press. "I don't know what their game is, but they are constantly following me around," he once said of his bodyguards. Another time, he and Harry invited themselves into a hotel room to watch as journalists edited footage of one of the princes' ski holidays in Klosters. Judging from the way the two princes were giggling, they found the procedure highly amusing.

Harry, who loves a good practical joke, once decided to surprise his brother during a cross-country race at Eton. He ambushed William by jumping out from behind a tree and pretending to be an autograph hunter. Harry thought it was hilarious, but William was not amused — perhaps because the joke was a little too close to reality for comfort.

EIGHT

# Being a Royal Teen

BY NOW, you may be wondering if you have the stamina to be a young royal. Certainly, in the British royal family, this is a job for life. It's not as though you can wake up one morning and say, "I don't feel like being royal today." In 2000, Princess Alice, the wife of the late Duke of Gloucester, one of the Queen's uncles, became the first British royal to officially "retire." She was 98! At the age of 100, Britain's Queen Mother was still fulfilling her royal engagements.

European monarchs don't view being a sovereign as a lifelong avocation in the same way that British royals do. They do abdicate — give up the throne — from time to time to allow their children to take over. In 1948, Queen Wilhelmina of the Netherlands stepped down in favor of Queen Juliana, and in 1980, Queen Juliana stepped down in favor of Queen Beatrix. But ever since Britain's Edward VIII gave up the throne to marry the woman he loved, abdication has been a touchy subject in the British royal family, and Queen Elizabeth II is not expected to step down in favor of her son Prince Charles. He, like Victoria's oldest son, Edward, will just have to wait. If the Queen lives as long as her mother has, Prince Charles could be pushing eighty before he ascends the throne. He has spent his whole life preparing for a role that he may execute for only a few years, months, or weeks — or maybe not at all.

## Waiting in the Wings

Queen Victoria lived to the ripe old age of eighty-one, and Prince Edward, her eldest son, had to wait until he was nearly sixty to become Edward VII. He once said: "I don't mind praying to the eternal Father, but I must be the only man in the country afflicted with an eternal mother."

So how does all this affect you as a royal teenager? You can take it as a given that your most pressing concerns will not be whether one of your grandparents is about to abdicate or whether you'll still be opening hospitals when you are in your nineties. What you'll more likely be doing is balancing the perks of your position against the price you'll have to pay to enjoy them. Consider your vacations. Vacations are supposed to be a time to relax and unwind. Lovely as royal vacations are, you can never really "get away from it all." As teenagers, William and Harry have enjoyed winter holidays at exclusive ski resorts. The price they pay for their fun on the slopes is the scheduled — and not-so-scheduled — media breaks with the bevy of photographers who inevitably follow them around. (As Prince Charles and his sons are all good skiers, the photographers often have to arrive early to take a few lessons if they are to have any hope of keeping up with the royal party.)

As teenagers, William and Harry have also invited some of their closest friends to cruise the Greek islands with them. On more than one occasion, the multimillionaire banker John Latsis has offered his luxury yacht for the royal family's summer vacation. The 120-meter (400-foot) yacht, the third largest in the world, has room for ninety people on board. It has ten staterooms, a disco, a Turkish bath, and a swimming pool. It comes complete with its own helicopter, speedboats, and jet skis. For the royal summer holidays in the Mediterranean, the sun usually shines and the company is good — but you always have to be on guard in case a photographer with high-speed film comes racing past in a speedboat or lies in ambush above a beach with a telephoto lens at the ready.

Consider also your free time as a teenage royal. At seventeen, William was at the center of a set that enjoyed going to London pubs, nightspots, and fancy restaurants. When he attended his first dance in London, he had two detectives in tow. (How cool would that be?) And needless to say there were cameras everywhere, so he had to watch how he behaved. One newspaper even set up a hotline for girls to phone in with juicy bits of information about the prince. Talk about putting a damper on your evening! Lots of girls wanted to kiss William, but he didn't succumb — at least not that night.

Some of the people William hangs out with have admitted to using drugs, but he is scrutinized so carefully that he'd find it difficult to do this without the media catching on. Think of the fallout if the heir to the British throne were caught doing drugs. It would be a public relations nightmare. So, in addition to all the arguments about why drugs are bad for you, William is under enormous pressure not to experiment with them because of the unwanted publicity it would bring his family. (The people you associate with can definitely cause you headaches if you are a teenage royal. Crown Princess Victoria of Sweden ran into problems when the press linked her with a group of young students who had a reputation for rowdy, drunken behavior at glamorous Swedish ski resorts. This kind of publicity may have had something to do with the anorexia nervosa the teenage princess was battling in the late 1990s.)

In 2000, when twenty-one-year-old Lord Frederick Windsor was photographed sprawled on the steps of the Home House Club after a particularly rowdy party, he wrote an open letter of apology to the British people saying that he was sorry for his behavior and he knew he should be setting a better example. And he's only twenty-eighth in line to the throne!

If you are a young royal, dating is certainly complicated. For one thing, royal etiquette gets in the way. How smoochy can you get if your date always addresses you in a formal manner? Diana called Prince Charles "Sir" while they were going out and didn't call him by his first name until they were engaged. For another thing, there are those pesky detectives riding along in the back seat of the car or, if you're lucky, trailing you in a car of their own. Having your personal security guards in attendance would be like taking your parents along on your dates with you. Think of how much fun that would be!

When young royals are not enjoying fancy vacations or hanging out with their friends or going out on chaperoned dates, they — like most teenagers — will be at school, putting a final polish on their educations in preparation for an adult life of public duty. As we have already seen, holding high academic qualifications is not a prerequisite for being a royal. Britain's Edward VII was politically astute and a well-loved king despite his poor education. George VI was well respected by his people despite his uninspiring academic record at naval college. Both Edward VII and George VI went to Cambridge, and George's older brother Edward VIII went to Oxford, but none of these kings undertook a full course of study while they were at university.

Neither Queen Elizabeth nor Prince Philip attended university, so they gathered together a committee of people to advise them as to whether Prince Charles should go. Charles didn't really have the grades, but it was decided that he should attend Cambridge anyway. At first the university planned to custom-design a course for him, but Charles, much to everyone's surprise, put his foot down and said he wanted to pursue a regular course in anthropology and archeology. He later switched to history and graduated from Trinity College with a second-class degree, despite having his time at Cambridge disrupted by a term at the University of Wales and by a number of royal duties. Charles's younger brother Prince Edward also got a second-class degree in history from Cambridge. Neither Princess Anne nor Prince Andrew went to university.

The most academically accomplished of the British royals so far is William's cousin Lord Frederick Windsor. In England, when students are eighteen, they take final exams in three — and occasionally four — subjects. These final exams are called A levels. Lord Frederick Windsor took four A levels and passed every one of them with top marks. He won a place at Magdalen College, Oxford, to study classics. The next-best royal performance was by Princess Anne's son, Peter Phillips, who passed three A levels (getting one B and two Cs). Peter graduated from Exeter University with a degree in sports science.

These days, many royals from other parts of the world finish their educations at prestigious colleges in the United States or Britain. Jordan's Prince Feisel went to Brown in the States. Crown Princess Victoria of Sweden went to Yale, and her brother, Prince Carl Philip, studied at Kent School in Connecticut (which is also where the Hollywood actor Ted Danson went to school). Denmark's Crown Prince Frederik went to Harvard. Crown Prince Haakon of Norway attended the University of California at Berkeley. Prince Felipe of Spain, Prince Pavlos of Greece, Hereditary Grand Duke Guillaume of Luxembourg, and Prince Bernhard of the Netherlands all went to Georgetown University in Washington, D.C. Prince Philippe of Belgium, the Duke of Brabant, studied constitutional history at Oxford and political science at Stanford University in California. Queen Margrethe of Denmark is Europe's best-educated monarch. After graduating from high school, she studied at two different universities in Denmark, then at Cambridge University, the London School of Economics, and the Sorbonne in Paris.

By sending both Prince William and Prince Harry to Eton when they were thirteen, Prince Charles was ensuring that his sons had the best possible chance of pursuing university careers, should they wish to do so. Eton has an excellent academic reputation, but Charles also chose the school because he did not want his sons to repeat his own disastrous experiences at Gordonstoun. Gordonstoun is a spartan school in the wilds of Scotland that welcomes boys from all kinds of different backgrounds. By sending Charles there, his parents hoped to instil some steel into him and also to try once more to get him to mix with other boys.

Charles stuck it out at Gordonstoun, but he hated every minute of it. The boys slept in unpainted dormitories with bare floorboards. Their daily regimen included two cold showers and an early-morning run around the garden in shorts. The school program was designed to turn out people of strong character who were self-disciplined and physically fit. Although Charles has since remarked that he is grateful for the education he received at Gordonstoun — he said it gave "shape and form and tidiness to his life" — at the time he was miserable. He was teased mercilessly because of the size of his ears. (They are rather large. His parents were once advised to consider having them surgically pinned back, but they decided against it.) He was also pursued by schoolyard bullies who were eager to take on a future king. His only reprieve was a couple of terms in a school in Australia, where he welcomed the relative anonymity and thoroughly enjoyed the expeditions into the outback.

When it came to William and Harry, Charles agreed with the idea that the princes should learn to mix with others. But rather than expecting his sons to survive in a totally alien environment, he chose schools where they would be with boys whose backgrounds were closer to their own. That way, he thought, William and Harry would develop a sense of belonging and be able to forge friendships that could last them through the rest of their lives.

So that's a relief — if you were born royal in Britain today, rather than having to take freezing-cold showers and sleep with the dormitory windows wide open even on winter nights, you could go to an expensive boarding school where you wouldn't be the only one with a private detective sitting outside your classroom. And — get this — some of the other students would be even wealthier than you were. You'd be as near normal as you were ever going to get.

Eton is extremely traditional, which fits well with royal family values. The uniform of black tailcoat, waistcoat, pinstriped trousers, winged collar, and white bow tie was adopted in 1820 when Britain was mourning the death of King George III, and it has not changed since. The school was founded in 1440 by King Henry VI. It hasn't educated any kings yet, but it has educated nineteen British prime ministers. When William was a student there, about thirty of the other boys were either princes or members of the aristocracy.

## The Eton Test

When William and Harry were thirteen, they had to sit an entrance exam in order to get accepted to Eton. Here are the kinds of questions they would have had to answer. Why don't you take a moment to test yourself to see how you might have done?

- Briefly describe how a volcano is formed.

- What is the approximate percentage of nitrogen in normal air?

- Sound cannot travel through metal, water, wood, or a vacuum?

- Organisms use carbohydrates as their main source of energy, growth materials, vitamins, or water?

- Why did Charles I decide to rule without Parliament between 1629 and 1640?

As hoped, both William and Harry fit in well at Eton. William turned out to be an intelligent and studious boy. He passed twelve GCSEs (the exams British students take when they are sixteen), and although his results were not officially released, they are believed to be five As, in history and languages, and seven Bs, including math and science. (If William got a B in math, he was way ahead of his father, who always had enormous difficulties with this subject. Luckily for Charles, his father was not overly concerned about grades. Prince Philip once said: "Look, I'm only going to bother if you're permanently bottom....

Just stay in the middle, that's all I ask." Now wouldn't you like to hear your parents say that!)

After his GCSEs, William chose art history, geography, and biology for A level study. Along with his academic subjects, he also took cooking and motorcycle maintenance. In his senior years, he was elected to Pop, an elite boys' club within the school. When you are in Pop, you get to wear multicolored waistcoats and hound's-tooth trousers to set you off from the crowd. The members of Pop act as school prefects, enforcing discipline. They make sure the younger boys go to church (at Eton students attend church three times a week) and serve as ushers at school plays. They also have the authority to fine students who break school rules.

At school, William achieved good academic grades and a position of responsibility. And in the world outside, he had become something of a heartthrob. Way back in October 1995, when William was thirteen, *Teen* magazine had included a pullout poster of him in their October issue. This was a first for the British royals, who have traditionally had a rather stuffy image (even if Charles was at one time voted most eligible young bachelor in the world). William's popularity continued as he grew older. When he dropped in unexpectedly at an upper-class party during a polo match when he was seventeen, photographers snapped photos of him in designer sunglasses. This caused quite a kerfuffle at Buckingham Palace: in the photographs, William looked rather more like a jet-setter than the royal family was comfortable with. Sales of designer sunglasses rose, but the prince has not been photographed looking quite so flashy since.

Although as a schoolboy William seemed uncomfortable when the media caught up with him, his younger brother, Harry, took these encounters in his stride, sometimes donning sunglasses and a baseball cap for his sorties out of Eton and into town. If anyone happened to ask if he was Prince Harry, he would reply, "Sorry, mate. I'm Bob." Prince Harry's more relaxed approach to life gives him something in common with his great-aunt Princess Margaret. Once when Margaret misbehaved as a girl, she said to her mother, "Isn't it lucky Elizabeth's the eldest?" Both Harry and Margaret could enjoy the more laid-back lifestyle that comes from knowing there is an elder sibling between you and the throne.

In 1997, when William was fifteen and Harry was thirteen, their mother, Princess Diana, was killed in a car accident in Paris. The car in which she was riding was traveling very fast through a tunnel, and the driver had been drinking. At the time the car crashed, Diana and her boyfriend, Dodi Fayed, were trying to evade photographers who were hot on their trail. William had not been fond of the press before his mother died, and the way she died made it even harder for him to accept their constant presence.

Charles, William, and Harry became closer after Diana's death. It was obvious the boys enjoyed the country life Charles valued so highly, and Charles became more openly affectionate with his sons. That same year, father and sons traveled to Canada for a skiing holiday. William and Harry were greeted by ecstatic crowds of teenage girls. Their Vancouver hotel room was stocked with CDs by Savage Garden, Oasis, and Spice Girls. They toured a school in Burnaby and then went skiing in Whistler, tackling some of the mountain's toughest runs.

As time passed, William began to figure out a way to deal with the press. He complained about an inaccurate story in one newspaper and received a full apology. On his sixteenth birthday, he answered a list of

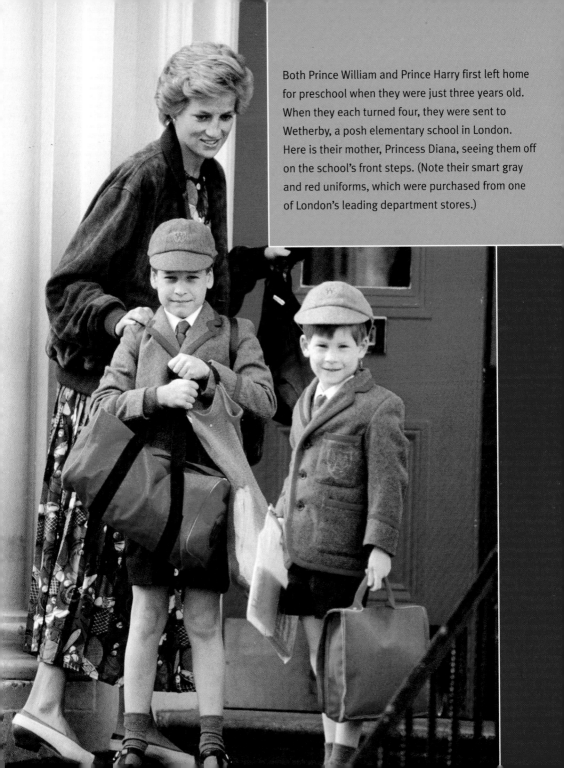

Both Prince William and Prince Harry first left home for preschool when they were just three years old. When they each turned four, they were sent to Wetherby, a posh elementary school in London. Here is their mother, Princess Diana, seeing them off on the school's front steps. (Note their smart gray and red uniforms, which were purchased from one of London's leading department stores.)

When Queen Elizabeth II was young, no one had any idea that one day she would be the queen. Here she is at the age of seven enjoying an exhilarating ride around a London park on her tricycle. Three years later, in 1936, her father unexpectedly became George VI after his older brother gave up the throne. As the new king and his family pose in their coronation robes (right), you can just tell that the lives of Elizabeth and her younger sister, Margaret, are about to change forever.

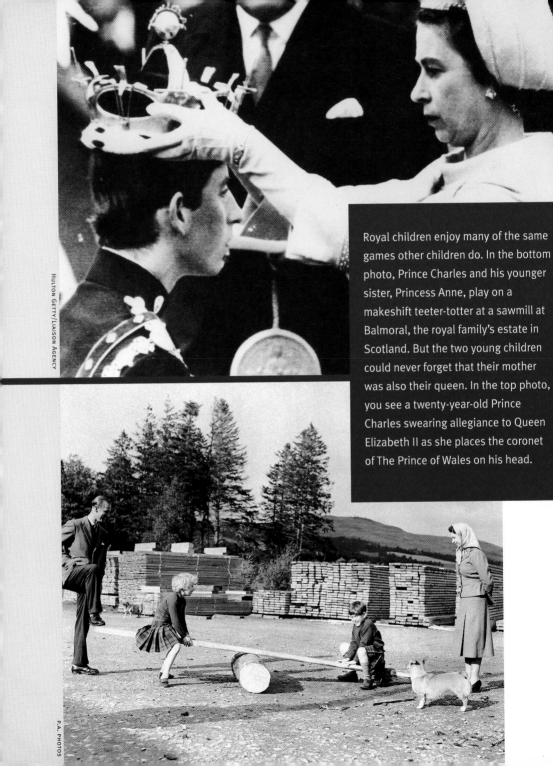

Royal children enjoy many of the same games other children do. In the bottom photo, Prince Charles and his younger sister, Princess Anne, play on a makeshift teeter-totter at a sawmill at Balmoral, the royal family's estate in Scotland. But the two young children could never forget that their mother was also their queen. In the top photo, you see a twenty-year-old Prince Charles swearing allegiance to Queen Elizabeth II as she places the coronet of The Prince of Wales on his head.

Imagine having to deal with a crowd like this every time you set foot outside your front door! (These photographers were hoping to catch Princess Diana as she left the headquarters of the English National Ballet in London.)

No milestone is left unturned in the media's quest to document royal lives: in 1999, seventeen-year-old William posed for photographers after he passed his driver's test. (The big red L off the front of the car showed his learner's status.)

Both Prince William and Prince Harry have had to accept the media as a part of their lives. While the boys were at Eton, Harry often seemed to handle the attention better than his older brother. In this shot, taken in 1999, he appears relaxed as he shows off the school's distinctive uniform.

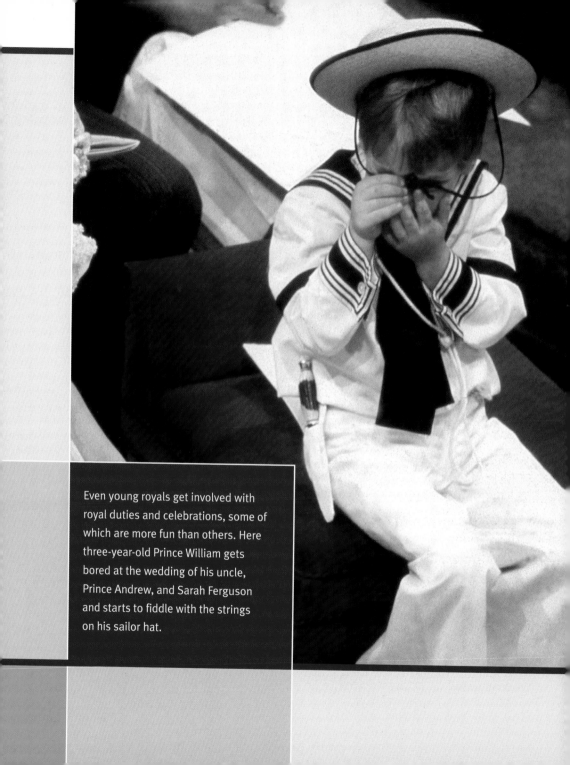

Even young royals get involved with royal duties and celebrations, some of which are more fun than others. Here three-year-old Prince William gets bored at the wedding of his uncle, Prince Andrew, and Sarah Ferguson and starts to fiddle with the strings on his sailor hat.

Six-year-old Prince Harry has a rather better time of it when he accompanies his father, who is colonel-in-chief of the Gurkhas, to watch the regiment go through their paces. To celebrate the occasion, Harry gets kitted out in a mini-uniform.

A king-to-be at work and play. Both these photographs were taken in 2000. In one, Prince William is playing on his school soccer team. In the other, he is varnishing shingles on a radio station in the remote Chilean community of Tortel as part of a volunteer community service project during a year off between school and university.

P.A. PHOTOS

P.A. PHOTOS

written questions, reporting that he liked reading (particularly action-adventure stories), sports, and action movies, but did not like being the center of attention.

## William at Sixteen

On his sixteenth birthday, Prince William answered written questions from the media. He would not answer any questions about girls or his friends, but here's what he would say. At sixteen William

- liked horses and fast food
- liked techno music and classical music
- liked modern clothes that he could buy for himself
- wanted to be sheltered from the glare of publicity
- did not feel comfortable with the adulation of teenage girls
- enjoyed solitary pursuits such as reading, and
- enjoyed playing computer games but did not have a computer of his own.

The palace also revealed that he had a flair for English and won a junior essay prize in 1992. He was a good tennis player, captain of his rugby and field hockey teams at school, and represented his school in cross-country running. He also swam, played soccer, and was a good shot.

The glimpses the public got of seventeen-year-old William showed him to be relaxed and courteous. On a geography field trip to Thornley, County Durham, he and his Eton classmates challenged the locals to a north-south karaoke competition. William and his friends gave an enthusiastic rendition of "YMCA" by the Village People, and the hotel owner tactfully declared the contest a draw. The owner of the hotel also said that William was very polite and returned the empty glasses from his table to the bar. In the Oystercatcher pub in Polzeath, Cornwall, that same year, William laughed it off when people began calling out the name Britney Spears. (Rumors were flying at the time that the prince and the pop star were sending e-mails back and forth.)

In the summer of 2000, William missed the joint celebration at Windsor Castle for the Queen Mother's hundredth birthday, Princess Margaret's seventieth, Princess Anne's fiftieth, Prince Edward's fortieth, and his own eighteenth because he was studying for his final exams. (Over 700 people attended his birthday bash without him.) His hard work paid off, and he got an A in geography, a B in history of art, and a C in biology, earning himself a place at St. Andrews, Scotland's oldest university. In the sixteenth century, many Scottish kings were educated there.

Students in Britain often take what is known as a gap year between school and university, and William was no different. He decided to devote his gap year to community-service work, environmental preservation, and adventure travel. His official companion for the year was thirty-four-year-old Mark Dyer, a former equerry to the Prince of Wales.

For the first part of his gap year, William dropped in for part of a grueling six-week training exercise with the Welsh Guards in Belize, a small country in Central America, to learn survival skills. He slept in a hammock in the jungle and ate army rations. (As a future Prince of Wales, Prince William has a particularly close connection with the Welsh Guards, a light infantry battalion raised by George V in 1915 to ensure Welsh representation among the country's foot soldiers. The regiment fought in both the First and Second World Wars and now takes part in active service and peacekeeping missions around the world.) After Belize, the prince hopped over to the island paradise of Mauritius in the Indian Ocean off the east coast of Africa. From there he traveled to Rodrigues Island, where he worked on a three-week marine conservation program with the Royal Geographical Society.

On September 29, 2000, after returning from Rodrigues, William gave the first major press conference of his life. He was rather nervous, and only a select group of journalists was invited. Although Prince Charles had endured intense media scrutiny from time to time during his school days, neither he nor his grandfather, George VI, gave an official interview to the press until they were twenty-one.

William dressed casually for the press conference in jeans, sneakers, and a fawn sweater. His father, at his side in a suit and tie, was there to lend moral support. Even though William's picture had been seen so often in all parts of the world, this was the first time his voice was heard in public. He talked of what he had done in Belize and Mauritius, and of his plans to continue on to Chile for more adventure travel and community service. He also revealed that he and Harry were upset by a recent book about their mother. They felt it betrayed Princess Diana's trust and showed that, even after her death, she was still being exploited by the media.

Following this meeting with the press, William left England for a ten-week trip to Patagonia with Raleigh International, an organization that sends volunteers on community projects around the world. Part of the requirement is that each volunteer raise his or her own funds for the trip. William raised $8,000 by holding a sponsored water polo match, enough money to both secure his own spot on the expedition and enable a volunteer from a youth development program in the north of England to join the group.

The Patagonia expedition included 110 volunteers aged seventeen to twenty-five from a wide variety of countries and backgrounds. In addition to people from Britain, there were volunteers from the United Arab Emirates, Hong Kong, New Zealand, Ireland, and Australia. Twenty-seven of them came from Raleigh International's at-risk program, which includes young people who are homeless or overcoming drug problems.

The volunteers kayaked along the coast of Patagonia, getting stranded on a remote beach for five days in the driving rain. They spent time at a national reserve where they studied Andean deer. Then they took a bus to Tortel, an isolated village 1,600 kilometers (1,000 miles) south of Santiago, where they helped restore buildings and build wooden walkways between the houses. Journalists came home loaded down with photographs of William sanding shingles on a schoolhouse and trying to explain to the children in Tortel what a wombat is. (Wombat is Charles's nickname for William.) William tried to draw one for the children, but his picture looked more like a knobbly potato than the Australian marsupial. At eighteen, William gave the impression of being a confident young man well equipped with the skills he would need as a future king.

His brother, Harry, has also grown more assured as the years pass. Although he is a joker who hams it up for photographers and a daredevil who was caught on camera in 1998 rappelling down a dam in Wales without a helmet, Harry also values his privacy, and he has no intention of becoming public property. Unlike William, Harry remained silent on his sixteenth birthday.

The teenage years are years when people start to think about just what it is they want to do with the rest of their lives. They experiment with all sorts of different interests to find out what they are good at, and they begin to think of possible careers and how their lives might unfold. The lives of royal teens are in many ways more restricted than the lives of other teenagers, because their roles have already been mapped out for them long before they were even born. As a royal teen, you will be royal and you will perform official royal duties. You will open up your life to public display, and people will have expectations that you will be expected to fulfil. Prince William's aunt, Princess Anne, once said that she never asked to be born a princess. Prince William and Prince Harry did not ask to be born princes, either, but they have learned that when you are royal, there is not much point wishing you were something else. As a royal teen, you might as well salvage whatever privacy you can and get on with the job that will be yours for life.

NINE

# Is This for You?

AS YOUR TEENAGE YEARS draw to a close, you begin to officially step out of the shadows. You are expected to leave childish ways behind and embrace a more formal lifestyle. Outside Britain, some European royal families are doing what they can to help more distant family members drop out of the royal limelight. In the 1980s, the Netherlands passed a law limiting the size of the official royal family, effectively allowing those not directly in line for the throne to pursue more normal lives. And other European royal families do not find the limelight so blinding as it is in Britain. Denmark's Queen Margrethe can walk into a store without causing a commotion. King Carl XVI Gustav and Queen Silvia of Sweden have flexible official schedules that are worked out mere weeks in advance. Grand Duke Henri of Luxembourg is left in peace by his people and can go about whatever royal duties he has without being hounded by the media. None of these monarchies, however, has the dazzle of the British royals. If you decide you'd like to be born into the British royal family, you cannot be a shrinking violet who seeks sanctuary behind castle walls. You'll have to be — or learn to become — comfortable with spending most of your life on display.

Once he turned eighteen in the summer of 2000, William could expect to be called "His Royal Highness." He has, however, asked for this honor to be delayed. He doesn't want to be curtsied or bowed to or called "Sir" just yet. In time, he will accumulate a row of titles like his father, who can call himself — amongst other titles — His Royal Highness Prince Charles Philip Arthur George, The Prince of Wales and Earl of Chester, Duke of Cornwall, Duke of Rothesay, Earl of Carrick, Lord of the Isles and Baron Renfrew, Prince and Great Steward of Scotland, Knight Companion of the Most Noble Order of the Garter, and Great Master and Principle Knight Grand Cross of the Most Honourable Order of the Bath. Charles is also personal aide-de-camp to Queen Elizabeth II; Commander Royal Navy; Wing Commander Royal Air Force; Colonel-in-Chief of ten regiments; president, patron, or member of some 200 clubs, charities, committees, and learned organizations; and member of a dozen or so international orders of chivalry.

If you are a young royal, there will always be official acknowledgments of your passage into adulthood. Madame Tussaud's, the famous waxworks museum in London, has decided not to make a wax figure of William until he is twenty, in case he grows more before then. But a new coat of arms was commissioned for him on the occasion of his eighteenth birthday.

Remember all that stuff about constitutional monarchies at the beginning of this book? As William takes on a greater role in public life, he will have to be careful to stay out of politics. When his father, Prince Charles, was at Cambridge, he thought that if he joined *all* the political clubs at university this might save him from accusations of political bias. But palace officials would not allow him to join a single one of

# William's Coat of Arms

Coats of arms started in medieval times when knights suited in shiny armor needed some way of identifying each other on the battlefield. A coat of arms is usually in the form of a helmet and shield decorated with images that reflect the family history or the family name. There may be a motto at the bottom and a crest at the top. Different colors, patterns, and animals each have their own heraldic significance. The shields of noble families may also have supporters on either side. William's coat of arms, which is based on his grandmother Queen Elizabeth's, has a lion (the national emblem of England) on the left and a unicorn (signifying Scotland and extreme courage) on the right. William's variations on the Queen's coat of arms make a personal statement. One of his additions was a small red scallop shell in memory of his mother. The shell, a popular symbol for medieval pilgrims, has been part of the Spencer coat of arms since the sixteenth century. William's coat of arms will change when he becomes The Prince of Wales to reflect his change in status. It may be a while before that happens, though — his father will likely become king first.

them, as even membership in the clubs might be interpreted as a political statement. William will have to deal with similar restrictions on his activities, and he will also have to be cautious about how he expresses his views in speeches and in letters. One time when Prince Charles drafted a letter to a church leader on a sensitive issue, the draft was returned to him by a private secretary with the note, "On no account is this letter to be sent." Palace officials have a responsibility to the government as well as to the royals, and they work to ensure that members of the royal family do not overstep their constitutional roles. William's palace-minders will be constantly watching to make sure the prince does not stir up trouble.

One of the most challenging areas for you as a royal as you mature may well be your choice of a lifelong partner. People who are born royal are trained for their roles from birth. This is one reason why it is so difficult to marry into a royal family these days and survive. One element in the mix must surely be the strain of suddenly being parachuted into the royal circle. The Empress Michiko of Japan, who was the first commoner to marry into the Japanese imperial family when she married Crown Prince Akihito in 1959, received an extremely frosty reception from her mother-in-law, Empress Nagako. Perhaps because of this, Michiko's son, Crown Prince Naruhito, had difficulty finding a bride. When Naruhito did finally marry, at the age of thirty-three, his bride, Masako Owado, wore a small ceremonial sword during the wedding ceremony. This is primarily a symbol of protection, but it is also a symbol of an earlier age in which, if an imperial wife brought dishonor to the family, she was expected to take her own life.

If the royal chooses a husband or wife from another country, the strains can be even more severe, especially if the countries do not have a history of cordial relations. Queen Beatrix of the Netherlands, for instance, married a German who had served in the German army during the Second World War. Since Germany had occupied the Netherlands during the war, it is hardly surprising that the Dutch were not thrilled about their queen's choice. Prince Claus has had to work hard to become accepted by his adopted nation. Queen Margrethe of Denmark encountered slightly different problems when she married a French aristocrat in 1967. In order to marry the Danish queen, Henri de Monpezat had to give up his nationality, his language, and his religion. In this case, however, he must have felt that the sacrifices were worthwhile, as Prince Henrik and Queen Margrethe have enjoyed a long and happy marriage.

The British royal family has been described as the world's most formidable in-laws. In a survey conducted in Britain in September 2000, Prince William was the least popular choice of roommate for people aged eighteen to thirty, because they said they would dread royal family visits. Although *Tatler* magazine voted William the world's most eligible single in 1991, in an October 2000 poll of Britain's most eligible bachelors compiled by *Star* magazine, he placed sixth, behind the son of British prime minister Tony Blair.

As William enters into more serious relationships, he'll have to bear in mind that, as heir to the heir to the throne, there are strict rules governing the kind of person he can marry. Under the 1701 Act of Settlement, he is barred from marrying a Roman Catholic. Under the Royal Marriages Act of 1772, if William marries before he is twenty-five, he will have to have the permission of the sovereign. As future supreme governor of the Church of England, he cannot marry someone who is divorced or who has a dubious past. In 2000, Norway's Crown Prince Haakon announced that he was living with an unmarried single mother and former waitress whose ex-husband was in jail for drugs. This kind of relationship will likely not be an option for William. Although all these rules sound daunting, bear in mind that young royals in Britain have it much easier now than they used to. In the old days, royal marriages were made to cement political alliances between countries, and British princes were expected to choose their mates from available Protestant princesses in Europe. (The role of British princesses was mainly to be married off to European princes.) As there aren't that many royal families left in Europe these days, commoners (people who are not born royal) now make acceptable royal spouses.

William, as a king-in-waiting, cannot expect that anyone he chooses will be thrilled to be his wife. It's one thing to get excited about dating the future king of Britain. It's quite another thing to seriously contemplate marrying him. The pressures of being the queen of Britain would give even the most devoted admirer pause for thought. Bertie (later George VI) had to ask Elizabeth Bowes-Lyons (now the Queen Mother) three times before she would agree to marry him, and Charles was turned down at least once before Diana agreed to become his wife.

Once you become a royal adult, you will have much royal business to attend to, but you will still have some free time on your hands. Perhaps you could devote it to building up a collection of some sort? Edward VII had a fine collection of walking sticks. George V collected stamps. Princess Margaret collects sea shells. And Prince Charles has a pretty nifty collection of toilet seats. Maybe there is a special hobby you would like to pursue instead. Queen Margrethe II of Denmark designs her own clothes. His Royal Highness Prince Khalid Al-Faisal bin Abdul Aziz Al-Saud, the son of the late Saudi Arabian king Faisal, is a painter who recently had an exhibition of his work in London. Emperor Akihito of Japan is an expert on freshwater tropical fish and regularly writes scientific papers about them. And the father of the current king of Sweden was an expert on Chinese porcelain.

William has not yet undertaken any royal tours on his own, but if you are a brother, sister, child, or grandchild of a king or queen (or are married to anyone who falls into these categories), you will likely find yourself traveling to promote friendly relations between your country and others. A royal tour may look like an opportunity for an all-expenses-paid vacation, but for those behind the scenes it is a major operation in logistics. There may be up to two tonnes (tons) of luggage (all pieces numbered, so that in case of emergency a required outfit and its accessories can be quickly located) and up to twenty accompanying staff. There will be carefully labeled presents for the hosts; popular gifts are signed royal photographs in silver or leather frames. (You will also receive gifts on your royal tours, and not all of them will be lavish. In 1958, a small Ethiopian prince, son of Emperor Haile Selassie, was surprised when he received a parting gift from Britain's Prince Henry. The boy rushed away and soon came back bearing presents for Henry's sons, William and Richard: two palace ashtrays. Princess Alice, William and Richard's mother, just hoped the emperor would not think the young British princes had stolen them.)

Before you embark on a royal tour, an advance party will scout out your accommodations and will make last-minute adjustments to suit individual royal preferences. For example, Prince Charles doesn't sleep well unless his bedroom is pitch dark, so heavy curtains in his bedroom are a must. Princess Diana used to be disturbed by noise, so her bedroom needed to be quiet. Your job, as the royal on display, will be to smile and wave and not complain if your feet hurt or if you have a headache.

There are definitely some tricks to be learned when undertaking royal tours. When Queen Elizabeth and Prince Philip toured Australia in the 1950s, the Queen, who was unused to the strong Australian sun, had to remember to lift her pearls every once in a while so that she wouldn't end up with a white line around her neck at the end of the day.

Although the royal yacht, *Britannia,* was taken out of service in 1997 as an economy measure, you will still have the British royal train and the royal flight to transport you on your travels. Royals don't usually take public transit, although Charles did ride a bus when he went

# Unofficial Mishaps

Princess Alice, who was married to one of Queen Elizabeth's late uncles, writes in her memoirs of the official duties she and her husband, Prince Henry, had to undertake when he was governor-general of Australia in the 1950s. As she discovered, unofficial events sometimes intruded on official ones. Just as Prince Henry was conferring a knighthood on one elderly gentleman, there was the sound of claws scrabbling on the wooden floor, and a mouse shot out in front of the royal party — closely followed by a tabby cat. The audience laughed and the knight-to-be, who had his back to the action, must have wondered if he'd done something terribly embarrassing like splitting his pants. On another formal occasion, a young child in the audience swallowed a marble and his mother had to hold him upside down until it fell out.

The food and accommodations sometimes left something to be desired as well. At one royal reception, Princess Alice was warned by her lady-in-waiting to avoid the iced coffee, as she had just seen it being made in a washing machine! On a particularly uncomfortable stopover, Princess Alice reported, there were crocodiles in the pool from which the drinking water was drawn and huge spiders all over the place. To top it off, the mattresses the royal family was given to sleep on were lumpy and turned out to be stuffed with cows' tails. There were compensations for the traveling royals, however. When the royal couple visited Ceylon (now Sri Lanka), Princess Alice had the rare honor of sitting on the knee of the sacred elephant that had carried the Buddha's tooth in the celebratory procession. She reported that the elephant was "kindly and obliging."

to his first school. Queen Elizabeth and her sister, Margaret, were taken on the London subway by their governess when they were young, just for the experience. During the First World War, Princess Marie-Louise once asked her cousin George V whether he felt it would be acceptable for her to take the bus as she had no car and taxis were scarce. He considered this carefully for a moment and then said: "What would Grandmama [Queen Victoria] have thought! But I think you are quite old enough to travel by bus. Do you strap-hang?"

Prince Charles and his father, Prince Philip, both qualified pilots, have been known to take the controls of airplanes that transport them to royal functions. His staff were not overly impressed the day Prince Charles landed the plane he was flying on one wheel. But quite apart from the possible danger of traveling with Charles, you should be aware that even the warm welcomes extended to royals sometimes carry risks. A cannon ball shot as a royal salute by Lord Newborough across the Menai Straits in Wales in 1911 almost sank the royal boat whose arrival it was celebrating. And sometimes there may be reasons beyond the purely practical for your method of transportation. When Prince Henry made his annual visit to Wellington College to hand out school prizes, he chose to travel by helicopter because he knew how much the boys liked to see their parents' hats blown off!

Once you are old enough to control your own royal budget, you must be seen to be using your money wisely and well. Income earned from British royal estates (with the exception of the Duchy of Cornwall, which belongs to The Prince of Wales) goes to the government, which then gives the royal family a set amount of money to live on each year. (This is known as the Civil List.) Increasingly, the royal family is doing what it can to raise extra funds. Sandringham, Balmoral, and the Duchy of Cornwall have all been registered as trademarks and labeled items are now for sale.

In this same spirit, Queen Elizabeth has opened up Buckingham Palace to paying visitors. Prince Charles took the tour and reported that he was very impressed. He even told a visitor he met in the palace gift shop that the tour of the royal home was better than visiting the Millennium Dome. (The Millennium Dome is a huge dome constructed on the River Thames to celebrate the year 2000. It contains many different exhibits and is now a popular tourist attraction.) The Queen originally opened Buckingham Palace to raise money for the restoration of Windsor Castle, which was badly damaged by a fire in 1992.

Not that you will be exactly poor as a British royal, of course. From Queen Elizabeth and then his father, Prince Charles, Prince William will inherit, among other things, two castles, two palaces, several country mansions, stables, thoroughbred horses, a race course, art treasures, stamp collections, libraries, antiques, and jewels. Once he becomes The Prince of Wales, he will receive income from land rents and mineral rights for tin mining, as well as 800 hectares (2,000 acres) of forest, the Oval cricket ground in London, 900 London flats, several pubs, a golf course, and some oyster beds. As The Prince of Wales, William will have the right to receive an annual tithe of 300 puffins from the Scilly Isles. And he will have first rights to any whale or porpoise that washes up on the Cornish coast. (This also means that he will be responsible for disposing of the carcass — an unexpected royal duty, perhaps, but a royal duty nonetheless.)

As you consider whether being royal is the career for you, remember that you will never be free from dealing with the stresses of royal duties. Of course you must try not to let them get to you — but if they do, try not to worry. Even seasoned hands like Prince Charles sometimes lose it. After one week of intense activity, he wrote this memo to his staff: "I didn't mean you to remove that glass for my toothbrush. It was a <u>particularly</u> nice glass. <u>Please</u> bring it back. If they have removed it I shall be very angry indeed. C."

Royal families exist at the will of the people, and the more the people respect you, the more they will want to keep you. As a royal you may be born into a position of privilege, but that position will not necessarily last forever. Your public will be constantly scrutinizing your performance and asking if you are worth all the money that is being spent on you. For instance, Britain's Princess Anne has a reputation for being abrupt, and her subjects do not appreciate what they interpret as bad manners. In contrast, the Queen Mother never fails to delight the people she meets. One day a boy of six was presented to her. He said, "Ma'am, I've also met your daughter. Do you know, she's *the Queen*." "Yes, I know," the Queen Mother replied. "*Isn't* it exciting!" In a poll conducted in December 2000 for the *News of the World* newspaper, Prince William was voted the most useful royal with a score of 7.4 out of 10. The Queen Mother came in second with 7.1. The royal who came last was the most recent addition to the family, Prince Edward's wife, Sophie Rhys-Jones. She scored a dismal 4.3.

So, remember that as you live your royal life, your public will always be there, watching you and giving you marks for your performance, even when you are not officially on duty. Imagine this. It's a bright sunny day. You have just arrived from the city, where you were dressed up in your formal best, waving to crowds from the palace balcony while people cheered and planes screamed through the sky, flying past the palace in formation. The day ended with a formal dinner at which uniformed staff served visiting dignitaries from dishes of the finest china. Today, you wake up in the comfort of your own bed at your royal country estate. What could be better, you ask yourself, than to take your dog for a long, relaxing walk down by the river. As you stroll along the riverbank, your dog rushes back and forth, begging you to throw sticks for him to chase. This is a lot more fun, you think, than shaking the hands of all those people you hardly knew and may well never see again. You bend down to pick up a short, sturdy stick, feeling the sun's warmth on the back of your neck. Suddenly, you hear a rustling in the bushes on the other side of the river. You catch the glint of sunlight on a telephoto lens. Instinctively you jerk back and turn away, but it's too late. As you hear the click of the shutter, you have a sinking feeling in the pit of your stomach. Tomorrow your photograph will be plastered over the newspapers for all the world to see.

Is this what you expected it would be like if you were royal? As you ponder this question, ask yourself if you think it would be better to be born into the British royal family, where you get lots of attention but where many demands are made in return, or if it would be better to be born into a European royal family that has dispensed with elaborate formal ceremonies, moved out of its palaces into cozier quarters, and no longer wants to be curtsied or bowed to. Finally, after all you've learned, do you still want to swap your life for the life of a young royal today? It's up to you to decide.

# The Royal Families
# of Europe

AT THE BEGINNING of the twentieth century, the map of Europe looked very different from how it looks today. Many countries in central and eastern Europe were part of the Austro-Hungarian and Russian empires, and the country we now know as Germany was made up of small sovereign states. In 1905, France, Switzerland, and San Marino (an independent state surrounded by Italy) were the only countries in Europe that did not have monarchies.

Then one by one, the sovereigns began to fall. The Portuguese had a revolution in 1910 and drove out their king, Manuel II. The end of the First World War in 1918 also saw the end of Charles I, emperor of Austria and king of Hungary, and of the Russian tsar, Nicholas II. The sovereigns of the German kingdoms of Bavaria, Prussia, Saxony, and Württemberg were either deposed or abdicated, and King Nicholas I fled Montenegro when it was annexed to Yugoslavia.

The upheavals continued with the Second World War. In 1939, Italy invaded Albania, driving out King Zog. Peter II of Yugoslavia lost his throne in 1945. Then in 1946, the Italians voted out King Umberto II, and the Bulgarians voted out King Simeon II. The next year, King Michael of Romania was forced to abdicate. The Greek monarchy survived some ups and downs until a military takeover in 1967, when King Constantine was forced to flee. He finally lost his throne in 1974, when the Greeks voted against inviting him back. By the end of the twentieth century, only ten royal families in Europe still had countries to rule: Belgium, Denmark, Liechtenstein, Luxembourg, Monaco, The Netherlands, Norway, Spain, Sweden, and the United Kingdom of Great Britain and Northern Ireland.

## Belgium

The sovereign of Belgium is His Majesty King Albert II. He is married to Her Majesty Queen Paola, an Italian aristocrat. Their oldest son, His Royal Highness Prince Philippe, Duke of Brabant, is the heir to the throne. The Belgian royal family is the poorest royal family in Europe. It has no fortunes, no jewels, and no art collections, but it does have a villa in the south of France for summer vacations.

## Denmark

The sovereign of Denmark is Her Majesty Queen Margrethe II. She is married to His Royal Highness Prince Henrik, a French aristocrat. Their oldest son, His Royal Highness Crown Prince Frederik, is the heir to the throne. Queen Margrethe is an informal monarch who holds fortnightly audiences with subjects who want to meet her and does all her own shopping (except for groceries). The family owns a chateau and vineyards in the south of France for summer relaxation, and a separate palace in Denmark that they use as a Christmas and Easter getaway. There is also a royal yacht, and the queen owns lots of jewels.

## Liechtenstein

Liechtenstein is a principality of 158 square kilometers (61 square miles) situated in a valley between Switzerland and Austria. As it is a principality rather than a kingdom, the ruler is a prince, not a king, and he has the title "His Serene Highness" rather than "His Majesty." The sovereign of Liechtenstein is His Serene Highness Prince Hans-Adam II. He is married to Her Serene Highness Princess Marie, a Bohemian countess. Their oldest son, His Serene Highness Hereditary Prince Alois, is the heir to the throne. The sovereign of Liechtenstein is one of the richest people in Europe, and the royal art collection is one of the best private collections in the world.

## Luxembourg

The Grand Duchy of Luxembourg is 4,144 square kilometers (1,600 square miles) of land where France, Germany, and Belgium meet. As Luxembourg is a grand duchy rather than a kingdom, the ruler is a grand duke, not a king. The sovereign of Luxembourg is His Royal Highness Grand Duke Henri. He is married to Her Royal Highness Grand Duchess Marie-Teresa, an extremely wealthy Swiss commoner. Their oldest son, His Royal Highness Hereditary Grand Duke Guillaume, is the heir to the throne. This family is the least expensive royal family in Europe to maintain. Their official residence is the 200-room Colmar-Berg Castle, forty kilometers (twenty-four miles) from the center of Luxembourg. When the family is not attending to royal duties, they enjoy a relaxed family life with lots of water sports, riding, skiing, and hunting.

## Monaco

Roughly the size of London's Hyde Park, the principality of Monaco is situated on a rocky outcrop overlooking the Mediterranean between France and Italy. As Monaco is a principality rather than a kingdom, its sovereign is a prince, not a king. The sovereign of Monaco is His Serene Highness Prince Rainier III. He married Hollywood movie star Grace Kelly, who was killed in a car accident in 1982. Their oldest son, His Serene Highness Prince Albert, Marquis des Baux, is the heir to the throne. The Grimaldis have ruled Monaco for over 700 years, making them the longest-ruling royal family in Europe. Monaco is famed for the casino at Monte Carlo, and outside of the United Kingdom, it has one of the most colorful and glamorous royal families in Europe. Prince Rainier's daughters, Caroline and Stephanie, often make the newspapers with their jet-setting lifestyles and turbulent love lives. Family holidays include winters in the Caribbean or skiing in Colorado.

## The Netherlands

The sovereign of the Netherlands is Her Majesty Queen Beatrix. She is married to His Royal Highness Prince Claus, a German diplomat. Their oldest son, His Royal Highness Prince Willem-Alexander, is the heir to the throne. From 1890 to 1967, this dynasty produced only queens, and Prince Willem is the first prince in over 100 years. This family is one of the most expensive European monarchies to maintain, and Queen Beatrix, with an estimated personal fortune of $3.33 billion dollars, is the wealthiest royal in Europe. There is a royal yacht and a royal train, and the queen has a good selection of jewels. Beatrix and her husband have a farm in Tuscany for the summer holidays.

## Norway

The sovereign of Norway is His Majesty Harald V. He is married to Her Majesty Queen Sonja, a Norwegian commoner. Their oldest son, His Royal Highness Crown Prince Haakon, is the heir to the throne. This is one of the least expensive European monarchies to maintain. The Norwegian royal family has a royal train with two carriages and a royal yacht, but when the king flew to Majorca for a yacht race in 2000, he traveled economy just like anyone else. The family owns two holiday houses on Oslo fjord, a mountain chalet, and a royal lodge where they spend Christmas.

## Spain

The sovereign of Spain is His Majesty King Juan Carlos. He is married to Her Majesty Queen Sofia, a Greek princess. Their oldest son, His Royal Highness Infante Felipe, Prince of the Asturias, is the heir to the throne. The Spanish royal family lives in the modest Zarzuela Palace, which used to be a hunting lodge. They eat out in restaurants, and the queen has no ladies-in-waiting. They like to ski and sail, and they take an annual summer holiday in Palma de Mallorca, an island in the Mediterranean.

## Sweden

The sovereign of Sweden is His Majesty King Carl XVI Gustaf. He is married to Her Majesty Queen Silvia, a German commoner. Their oldest daughter, Her Royal Highness Crown Princess Victoria, Duchess of Västergötland, is the heir to the throne. This is another low-maintenance European monarchy. There is a royal train, but it has only one carriage. In the 1980s, the family moved out of the 600-room

Stockholm Palace, which, at the time, was the largest inhabited palace in Europe. The Swedish royal family has one summer home on an island in the Baltic and another on the Riviera. They also own a ski lodge in Sweden. Of all the royal families in Europe, the Swedish royal family is the one with the least power.

### United Kingdom of Great Britain and Northern Ireland

The sovereign of the United Kingdom of Great Britain and Northern Ireland is Her Majesty Queen Elizabeth II. She is married to His Royal Highness Prince Philip, the Duke of Edinburgh. Their oldest son, His Royal Highness Prince Charles, The Prince of Wales, is heir to the throne. Queen Victoria, an ancestor of the present queen, is known as the grandmother of Europe, because so many of the European royal families are related through her. The British monarchy is one of the most expensive European monarchies to maintain. Although Queen Elizabeth II is often said to be the wealthiest woman in the world, it is difficult to estimate her fortune as many of the trappings of the British royalty — the palaces and castles and jewels — go with the position rather than the person and so they do not really belong to the Queen. The Queen's personal income is a private matter, and people can only guess at what she is worth. In 2000, she was estimated to be the nineteenth-wealthiest woman in the world.

# Author's Note

MUCH OF THE INFORMATION in this book comes from magazine and newspaper reports about royals. Two British magazines — *Majesty* and *Royalty* — are devoted to nothing but royal news. Both of these can be found at newsstands throughout Britain and North America, and many libraries subscribe to them as well. *Royalty* magazine also has a Web site at www.royalty-magazine.com. The *Royal Report,* a newsletter sold by subscription, also covers royal news. (*Royal Report* will e-mail you the *Royal Press Review,* a free electronic update of royal headlines, and provide you with links to other royal sites. You can contact them at www.royalreport.com.) *People* magazine and *Hello!* also provide tidbits of information about royal lives.

There are many sites on the World Wide Web that track royals. Most countries with monarchies have government sites with information about their royal families, and some royals have Web pages of their own. (A good place to start for the British royal family is www.royal.gov.uk.) Then there are sites set up by royal fans about particular individuals or aspects of royalty. For instance, www.heraldica.org runs the alt.talk.royalty newsgroup, devoted to discussions about royal families around the world. Many news sites, such as Yahoo! News, also have sections specifically devoted to royalty.

Libraries are full of books about royals. Here are a few of the titles I read while writing this book:

- Alice. *The Memoirs of Princess Alice, Duchess of Gloucester.* London: Collins, 1983.
- Boulay de la Meurthe, Laure, and Françoise Jaudel. *There Are Still Kings: The Ten Royal Families of Europe.* New York: Clarkson N. Potter, 1981.
- Bradford, Sara. *Elizabeth: A Biography of Her Majesty the Queen.* London: William Heinemann, 1996.
- Brody, Wendy. *Prince Harry.* New York: Pinnacle Books, 2000.
- Crawford, Marion. *The Little Princesses.* Newburyport, Mass.: Focus Publishing, 1993.
- Dimbleby, Jonathan. *The Prince of Wales.* London: Little, Brown and Company, 1994.
- Edgar, Donald. *The Queen's Children.* London: Arthur Barker, 1978.
- Holden, Anthony. *Prince Charles: A Biography.* London: George Weidenfeld & Nicolson, 1988.
- Hough, Richard. *Born Royal: The Lives and Loves of the Young Windsors.* New York: Bantam, 1988.
- Longford, Elizabeth. *Oxford Book of Royal Anecdotes.* Oxford: Oxford University Press, 1989.
- Longford, Elizabeth. *Elizabeth R.* Musson: 1983.
- Morrow, Ann. *The Queen.* New York: Morrow, 1983.
- Reisfeld. Randi. *Prince William: The Boy Who Will Be King.* New York: Pocket Books, 1997.
- Russell, Peter, and Paul James. *At Her Majesty's Service.* London: Collins, 1986.
- Seward, Ingrid. *Royal Children.* New York: St. Martin's Press, 1993.
- Talbot, Godfrey. *The Country Life Book of Queen Elizabeth The Queen Mother.* London: Country Life Books, 1978.

# Index

JANE BILLINGHURST grew up in a small village south of London. After graduating from Oxford University with a degree in Modern Languages and Philosophy, she moved to North America in 1982. She has lived on the east coast of the United States and the west coast of Canada. A freelance writer and editor of biographies and natural histories, she lives with her two daughters, Stephanie and Nicola. Like William and Harry, she has spent winter holidays in Orlando, Florida, and Whistler, British Columbia. She is the author of *Hey Girl! A Journal of My Life* (Annick, 2001), *Grey Owl: The Many Faces of Archie Belaney* (Greystone, 1999), and *The Spirit of the Whale* (Raincoast, 2000).